My Years Hidden

As a Boy

Iron Curtain Memoirs

Book 2

by

Irene Kucholick

Three Kings Publishing

Princeton, Kentucky

To my Mother and Nadja, without them, us kids would not have survived.

Acknowledgments

With many thanks to my good friend Sam Cooper, who spent much time, helping me greatly with research and general detail work. Also many thanks to Phyllis Hole who helped and worked with me to start this enormous amount of labor and urged me to go on when I wanted to give up. I want to thank my good neighbor Merlin Berry, who gave me many good tips and helped greatly over the last year. Thanks so much to my brothers Hartmut and Claus, (Ortwin died in i1961) who were able to dedicate their time and helped me with many details. But above all, I want to thank my husband, Walter P. Kucholick, who always gave me great encouragement.

My Years Hidden

As a Boy

AFTERMATH
1945 - 1947

The war was over! On May 6, 1945, I joined other youths in the village to celebrate. We laughed and talked about being able to walk around without watching for dive bombers. I sat in the middle of the Street and shouted, "Nothing can happen to me now. The war is over!" We heard that many high ranking Nazis, Hitler and Goebbels family had killed themselves. We knew they got what they deserved.

The five French POWs were taken away in a truck. Nadja wanted to go to France with Paul but was not allowed to do so. Paul told her he would come back for her. I did not realize how much they cared for one another until I saw them standing in a long embrace. Paul walked toward the truck only when ordered to do so by an officer. Nadja stood with tears streaming down her face, helpless and sad.

"Come back! Come back!" she cried as they drove away waving their tricolored flag. We could still hear their singing even after they were out of sight. We never saw them again.

As peace was declared, Russian tanks rolled through Euba. We were warned on the village blackboard to stay inside f or fear of being shot. During the night the Russians came. Hour after hour we listened to the squeaky rumbling of massive tanks vibrating our building. We stayed in bed, too afraid to even peer out of the darkened windows. We knew Germany was to be divided into four parts. The Americans got the south; the English the northwest; the French a part of the west;

and the Russians got the east. We knew the city of Berlin was also divided into four parts.

Since we were so hungry, we said among ourselves, "Russia is closer. They can bring in supplies much faster than the Americans. The Russian zone will do airight." We had been Cold for years that Russian farmers had fertile land and worked as hard as the German farmers. Once Papa had came back from the Russian front, he said, "Their farmland has beautiful black soil. When the war is over it will be the breadbasket of Europe." No one told us then that the Russians were starving. They were not able to feed themselves. They did not send us food, rather they took what little we had. People were confused and we knew more hard times were ahead.

When Stalin heard that so many people in Germany wanted democracy instead of communism he said, "What, they don't want to be communists?" He laughed. "We'll starve them and they will come crawling to us!"

Statements like this and other rumors began to make the rounds. No one knew what was ahead for Germany's defeated people. The feeling of uncertainty about our future was most evident in the constant stream of refugees still fleeing westward. It was called FLUECHTLINGSTRECK (Covered Wagon Trek). We could see them in the distance, the steady slow procession of people from early morning until late at night. The refugees often walked beside their horses seeming to talk to them as both man and beast seem strained to keep going.

We were told by the refugees coming through that we could take a document, which listed all our lost belongings and our destroyed store, to West Germany where we would be compensated. East

Germany will not make any restitutions and people have to be quiet about it of what they had lost in the war.

Borders between the zones were established and border guards were assigned to patrol them. A Russian commandant patrolled our streets. With a large dog trotting beside him, he strutted around our village acting like a king. The commandant then acquired a motor cycle and ripped the air with its accelerating motor. He also imposed an 8 p.m. curfew.

We requested and received from the State Farm a very small garden plot. It was late May and we looked forward to some fresh garden vegetables. We also planted a small patch of tobacco which we hoped to sell. The farm administrator gave us rutabagas, sugar beets and potatoes from their storage in exchange for working in the fields. We cooked and stirred diced sugar beets for hours to make a tangy black syrup (molasses). Nadja worked on the farm for her DEPUTAT (food-for-work-wage). English term: (Payment in kind) She would often slip something by for little Christine. Records were kept of the hours Ortwin and I worked. We were to be paid at harvest time.

All the DEPUTAT portions were measured according to the size of the family and very tight.

Early each morning Nadja and Mama picked leaves from the stinging nettles that grew along the edges of the fields. When picked early, these slender leaves were fresh and tender. If picked late in the day, they were tough. Mama made nettle soup that tasted like spinach but it quieted our stomachs for a while. There were many days we had nothing at all to eat.

The farmers hired guards to keep people from stealing food from their farms. Armed with horsewhips and clubs, men hired by the farmers rode bicycles around the fields or lay half concealed in the bushes guarding their fields 24 hours a day. They seemed to know we were picking leaves from the nettles and did not stop us but they watched us constantly. I remember a big sign at the corner of a farm, saying: "Thieves will be prosecuted."

People in the city suffered most. Only a few came to get something from the fields. If they were successful they ran for their lives back into the city. The field guards were masters with the whip.

Although we continued to receive ration cards, our stores had nothing to sell. Euba's general store sometimes sold grits and people ran to get in line, but it was never enough for everybody. We could however usually get vinegar and salt. Empty store shelves were filled with advertisements of things available before the war. The few stores in Chemnitz, not destroyed by bombs, were empty and the owners simply closed their doors.

There were some who had food enough, the farmers and the Russians who came to govern us. The Russians assigned to govern our village stayed in a villa up in the woods. A large red star on their roof was lit by spotlights during the night. They made their own parties, drinking vodka in large amounts, and played their music as loud as possible. Since the Russians also had their food rationed, they were always looking around the village for something extra to eat. While doing this they found out where women lived, then returned at night, abducted them and took them to their villa.

"FRAU, KOMM" (Woman, come) and "WO IST FRAU?" (Where is woman) were calls repeated over and over by Russians prowling our village streets until small children took up the sayings, not knowing the serious intent of our occupying intruders.

One night, after curfew, Nadja and I slipped through the darkness up to the Russian villa. We were very hungry and thought this might be a place to get some food. We stayed in the shadows of a picket fence and some bushes where the searchlights would not fall on us. Our hunger was greater than our fear of what the consequences would be if we were caught.

Several soldiers were cooking in a large pot out in the open. We could smell the meat. "Borscht" Nadja whispered. When they dumped a lot of vegetables into the pot my stomach cramped with hunger. They were singing and talking loudly as they drank their vodka and sang "Kathusha" and "Nabasitzia Djewuschka" over and over and over.

Finally they talked about finding women. After eating huge bowls of borscht, four men left to go into the village.

"After they eat, they sleep," Nadja whispered.

We waited. Some of the men went inside and apparently went to sleep. We waited and all was quiet.

To our astonishment three of the four soldiers came back with three women. They were the wives and daughters of the farmers, not the starving refugee women. These were the women who gave us that salt soup when we first came to Euba. These women had refused to give us even one potato when we were hungry and without a home. Usually these women hid in their barns but the soldiers ap rently knew this and had persuaded them with their guns.

"Let us go!" shouted a stoutly built woman. "You will be punished for this."

5

A soldier bellowed back at her in Russian. She said nothing more. One woman was slapped when she bit a soldier as he tried o put his arms around her. The three women huddled together and the guns kept them constrained.

"They wait for commandant," Nadja whispered. We waited. The commandant did not come. The soldiers divided the women and gestured to them that they would let them go after awhile. The man they called "Stachina" forced one of the woman into the house.

When they offered the two remaining women food, the women spit on it. If they had been one of the hungry people, they would have eaten it. The men drank and danced and laughed. They were like children. One by one each Russian grabbed one of the women and forced her into the house. When they protested they were slapped into a whimpering silence. I could feel no pity for them when they screamed and cried out. I could not forget that these were the women who had denied very small children even one bite of food when we came from Chemnitz.

"It soon be over. Wait more, they sleep," Nadja's voice was low. "We'll take food."

We heard the men fighting over one of the women. It must have been another hour before we were sure the men were sound asleep.

"Now!" Nadja whispered as she climbed out of the bushes and over the fence into the garden. I followed. Slowly, quietly, we crept toward the house. The kettle outside still had some warm borscht, in it.

We poured it into a pitcher we had brought, then crept into their kitchen. We took some big pieces of commisbread. I saw a box I could carry and took it, not daring to risk the noise of opening it.

A man cursed and we knew a soldier was awake. We held our breath in fear, then it was quiet and we heard snoring. He must a have been dreaming.

We knew the women were awake. One of them tried to cry out but her cry was muffled. Probably by a Russian's hand ... We doubted that the women could get away. Perhaps they thought we were their husbands coming quietly to rescue them. Carefully we picked our way out of the kitchen, through the moon lit yard and into the safety of darkness.

"Thank heaven their commandant did not return," I whispered.

"I can breathe much easier out here in the dark.""Yap," Nadja said taking my arm. "Hurry home."

When we arrived home with our food, everybody got out of bed. We sat down and ate bread and borscht. It was the first meal we had eaten except for one rutabaga in two days. The box I had taken was full of Knorr's Instant Soup mix.

"My guess is they stole it from the factory warehouse just outside of Dresden," Ortwin said.

This was the first of a few more dangerous trips to their villa. Our trips were not always successful but when our hunger was great we were able to take some food from their kitchen. We always took reasonable amounts to avoid suspicion.

The Russian soldiers constant search for women was greatly feared by women in Euba. When the women learned they could not be protected within their homes they left their children and slipped away to sleep in the trenches dug by German soldiers. The trenches were deep and fairly dry. Some trenches had small wooden sheds with straw floors which provided cold but fairly comfortable places o hide.

German men were afraid to protect their women from these assaults since they were not allowed to have weapons.

Refugees assigned to settle in Euba and in surrounding towns were offended by the Russians who grabbed their daughters and wives. They soon packed up and moved on to the Western zone.

German families gave many things to the Russian soldiers in the hope that they would not be molested. When they returned to Russia they took many of these things with them. We learned of one Russian colonel who took an entire boxcar of furniture, but it was all confiscated by the Russian government.

Russia had few of the then-modern things we used in Germany and the Russians wanted everything. Stalin did not like his soldiers coming back to Russia talking about the nice things they had seen in Germany. Watches and jewelry became "hot" items with the Russian soldiers. They suspected every German was hiding a watch somewhere. Grandpa Michael told us of a Russian taking an alarm clock to a jeweler and demanding that he make him two wristwatches from the parts of the alarm clock.

One day Ortwin carried home riding a new bicycle.

"Mama." He bent over in laughter. "A Russian traded me his new bike for my old one. He thought my old bike would be easier to ride. He didn't know it was his lack of skill that kept him from riding his new bike.

Ortwin was elated since his old bike was pieced together from — parts of bikes found in the rubble.

July and August brought a welcome harvest from our garden. Fresh cooked beet greens, onions, and tomatoes were followed by kohirabi and tiny new potatoes. These foods were delicious additions to our table. — Summer passed and the fall of 1945 brought an order we found hard to accept. All Ukrainians were to be gathered up and returned to Russia. This would include Nadja. Some Ukrainians became frightened about their future and ran to West Germany. We learned later they were put in camps for displaced persons. A few lucky ones made it to Canada but the majority of them were sent back to Russia, according to the Yalta agreement between Russia and the Allies.

For a few weeks we hid Nadja in an abandoned hut in the woods. One morning when I went up to take her some food, she was gone. Grief stricken, we thought we would never see her again.

A few weeks later Nadja returned, driving up to our barn with a horse and wagon.

Surprised and pleased, I ran to her shouting, "Mama!" Ortwin Here is Nadja, She's come home."

Joyous to see her, we had many questions. "Where did you come from? Why the horse and wagon? "We'll never let you go again!"

"I promise take horse and wagon back. We stay in villa, near Planitz Strasse. Many Ukrainian women there. We go back to Russia." Our joy was brief. We learned she could not stay with us. She had promised to return and they knew where she was.

"I'm going to come and see you Nadja," I promised. Her smile beamed all her love for us.

When she left she warned, "You come. Wait outside. They no see you. Like we go Russian Villa." She pointed toward the place we had taken food from the Russians.

With this arrangement I made several trips to see Nadja. A large garden with many shrubs and chestnut trees surrounded the villa. I found it easy to hang around outside, hiding until Nadja would see me then signal me to come closer. On one visit I found Nadja's eyes red and swollen from crying. All the women will be sent to Siberia rather than her previous home, Poltawa. "Stalin has given orders"....I dissolved in a flood of tears on her shoulder. Losing this dear friend was not going to be easy. My sadness was so great I was unable to give her the comfort she needed.

During other trips to see her, she was allowed to leave the villa for brief periods. We usually walked about and talked. Late one evening, while waiting to see Nadja, I watched some Russians drag a cow they had stolen and killed into a small clearing and start to butcher it. Nadja signaled for me to wait. While they were carrying some of the meat inside, Nadja and I rushed to the freshly butchered carcass. I carried a whole liver and she gave me another heavy piece of meat. Nadja carried other pieces. Hidden by darkness we ran across the fields, carrying our stolen prize all the way to Euba. Mama was happy to see the meat but shocked to see our bloody clothes. She embraced Nadja.

"We will miss you, Nadja. I'm going to awaken the boys so they can see you, but not before you take off those bloody clothes. You a girls would never have gotten all that meat here in the daylight. Look at yourselves. 0h" Nadja stayed with us that night so Mama could wash and dry her clothes. Nadja's clothes were very ragged. a Early the next morning, at Mama's suggestion, we took a piece of a our pirated meat and set out for Niederwiesa. We planned to trade the meat for a dress for Nadja. On the main Street of Niederwiesa we knocked on the doors of homes where people had not been bombed and asked if they were willing to trade a dress for meat. We soon found a family with a daughter Nadja's size. Nadja could choose among three dresses. She decided on a colorful pretty summer dress — and both parties were jubilant over the exchange. That morning Nadja and I parted to go our separate ways with the warmest feelings of friendship. One day I returned to the villa and found the building empty. A Russian soldier was sweeping the steps in front. I approached and said, "Where Frauleins?"

"Frauleins all go home to Russia." He smiled at me. I backed up as if struck. His blunt statement felt like a blow. His expression turned serious as he watched me. I turned and walked away. Tears blurred my vision and I stumbled against the gate. After a few moments I started my slow heavy-hearted journey home.

I felt so sad as I climbed the stairs to tell Mama the agonizing news. We all mourned Nadja's absence and like so many of our other friends, we never heard of her again. After Nadja was taken away, about that time we were moved into a two-room apartment on the second floor of a small white building which belonged to the farm.. We shared a bathroom with another family. Our garden plot was located behind this house and best of all, we moved away from the mice.

Ortwin and I worked in the fields after school hours and received a cup and a half of milk each day for Christine. Other than our garden produce, potatoes, sugar beets and rutabagas in small quantities, continued to be our diet. Now and then we managed to get an egg. Before time to go to school, Ortwin would lie down outside the chicken coop and watch the hens through a small hole. If an egg was laid, he pushed himself through the opening and took it. He would break it and drink it raw. When he found two eggs he brought one to

11

Mama. When we helped harvest the corn to make winter feed for the swine I husked an ear of corn and ate it raw. It was fresh and sweet. I liked it.

"Pig! Pig!" shouted the farm workers. I turned to see them pointing at me and laughing. "Irene eats food for pigs!"

I called them "dumb cows" because they did not know what they were missing . I liked the sweet taste of fresh corn and took some ears home with me. Mama would have none of it, saying, "It's pig feed, Irene." She dismissed the idea promptly.

Nevertheless, all during the harvest I ate fresh raw corn and I had no ill effects from it.

With Nadja gone, I never dared to take food again from the Russian villa. I most certainly would be caught had I gone up there alone or with my brothers. We just had to think of another way to feed ourselves. One day Mama said, "Irene, with your slight build you look more like a boy than a girl in those black SS trousers and your felt boots.

I laughed. "Maybe I should get a man's haircut."

"Not a man's cut but with a shorter cut and that cap pulled down, you'd look more like a 14 year old boy than a 16 year old girl."

"I'd feel a lot safer from the Russian soldiers if they thought I was a boy."

Thus I assumed the disguise of a boy. Mama cut my hair shorter and I kept part of it hanging over my forehead. The poorly fitted black pants and shirt, along with the oversized boots made it possible for me to look many a Russian in the eye and be mistaken for a boy. I often made it a point to have a runny nose to further my disguise. This pretense as a boy was to serve me well for a few years.

12

One night a Russian patrol on horseback came into the area where we lived. One of them knocked on the door, We opened the door and saw a big soldier smiling at us. He grabbed Mama. I thought my heart would stop beating. We knew immediately what would happen to Mama.. We screamed as loud as we could. Mama screamed too. Ortwin and Hartmut kicked him. With all the people living in that building, we thought someone would come to our aid, but they shut their doors tight and kept quiet.

By now five soldiers were standing in the open doorway. We raised so much commotion that their horses tied to the picket fence outside became frightened and bolted, pulling up a portion of the fence. Their horses ran wildly down the street.

Our unwelcome intruders left, now more concerned with their run-away horses than their sexual gratification. We could hear them swearing as they ran after their horses. We hoped they would never come back.

Our neighbors in the building were unhappy that the fence was broken and not at all concerned that a neighbor was in danger of being raped. From that night on, until we were discovered, Mama and I joined other women to sleep in the trenches.

A Russian troop maneuver early one dawn revealed our hiding place. We were routed out, cursed at, and sent home. Following this incident, soldiers were kept under more strict control. Even so, some soldiers continued to rape the women. On those nights when everything was quiet and we heard no "FRAU KOMM, FRAU KOMM" we would say, "Tonight the good ones are on patrol."

One day Mama sent me to Niederwiesa to get a few pounds of oat kernels ground. When I arrived, I went to the home of my friend

Ursel Kilian and asked her to show me where the mill was located. Ursel had lived in the town all her life and I was hoping that she would accompany me to the mill. Ursel told me of the danger of being outside. "Russian soldiers stop and force women into trucks. They take them to their barracks and make them scrub floors all day and rape them. At the end of the day they are given a bowl of grits and the lucky ones can walk home others are made to stay. They'll pick up anyone available of f the streets. Some even go willingly to get a bowl of grits."

"It's one way to get a little food," I said. "We all know our stomachs hurt most of the time. I must get the oats ground. We really need the food."

Ursel and her mother decided to go with me. We walked rapidly and made it to the mill with no problem. We had to wait in line to get the kernels milled. It was late afternoon when we started home and knew it would be after curfew before we could reach Frau Kilian's home.

At dusk a group of five Russians, patrolling on bicycles, passed us then turned around and began following us. We walked faster. They advanced and wheeled around us in a threatening circle from which we could not escape.

There was no doubt as to their intentions. They suddenly wheeled closer, dismounted and grabbed us by the shoulders. Would I be mistaken for a boy? Evidently so. I was to be taken care of first. A hard blow to my face sent me reeling dizzily backward. A sickening kick in my stomach knocked me down. Four of the men grabbed Ursel and her mother, forcing them to the ground. I tried to slip along the wall of the building, thinking the growing darkness would hide

14

my escape. A big hand on my neck shoved me against the bricks. I was warned not to move if I wanted to live. Another blow in my face and stomach left me in great pain and unable to move. I could only lie there and witness the sordid scene of rape.

They pushed the women's dresses up to their necks and tore their underclothes. The noise of the women's screams and male cursing must have been heard for some distance by many people, yet no one came to help. The lights went out in nearby windows and I knew people must have been watching from their darkened houses, afraid to intervene since the Russians were armed with guns.

The men laughed, knowing no one would come to help us escape their fiendish act. The men took turns climbing on the women while the others pushed their fists into their mouths, pinning them to the ground. Each soldier shifted from Ursel to her mother without even pulling his pants up.

When they finished their grunting and cursing they left, laughing about their monsterous acts of repeated rape. The air reeked with the odor of alcohol and garlic. The profanity and coarse laughter that blasted the air moments ago echoed in my mind. Ursel and her mother lay on the ground in agony. They looked like bundles of wet clothing. Ursel's mouth was bleeding and each groaned with pain as they sat up.

The curfew was already in effect and their home was about four blocks away. This distance proved to be a painful walk for all of us. Just as we turned into another street a second Russian patrol came on bicycles. Fearful, we started to run. I stumbled and fell which brought the Russians quickly in front of us.

After explaining our situation, the Russians walked the remaining distance with us to protect us from more violence. We just had the misfortune to encounter a bad patrol before them. I still had my bag of oats. As they had not taken it from me.

I slept at Ursel's home because of the late hour and because I was in much pain from the blow to my face, stomach and other places of my body. The next morning I was horrified to see our swollen and bruised faces. When they told me this kind of attack had happened to them before, I hid my face in my hands and cried.

"Don't feel bad, Irene, we'll go to the hospital today."

When I arrived home, Mama wept as she washed my black eyes and swollen face. We were grateful my male disguise had saved me from being raped.

"I'm so sorry for Ursel and Frau Kilian. I am to blame for what happened. I'll never let you go there again."

Fall passed and winter came. If we had not looked at the calendar we would not have known it was Christmas 1945. We had a few sacks potatoes and very little else to keep us going, but the people in the city did not even have that. They were starving badly. Typhoid fever reached the epidemic stage even though everyone in the city was vaccinated.

I began scouting further from home in the hope of finding more food. With few rations available and money worthless, it took large sums to buy food in the black market. One pound of butter cost 200 Reichsmark, equivalent to fifty 1946 U.S. dollars.

It was the same year, when the communist party put out a resolution of the people, demanding that all the big firms, plants, businesses and farms be given to "the people". Once that was done, all the capital of the city was confiscated and now was owned by the state. The repayment to Russia started. Those plants that had worked for the economy and later for the war, now worked for Russia. The German people were told that it all belonged to "the people". But if a person would take as much as one pencil from their working place, they were branded as an enemy of the people the communist party and peace, and lost a good position if they had one. I knew farmers who lost their farms with every animal on it. It did not belong to them anymore but they were now allowed to work as farmhands on their own farm. The same thing happened with hotels and many other businesses. Many people, who had build up their businesses for generations, did not want to give them up. Those people perished, no one knew where they had been taken.

I spent more time with my friend, Krista Neubert, the daughter of one of the foremen from the state farm. Krista was my age, the same height, and her blue eyes contrasted with my brown ones. She wore her light hair in two long braids. Krista's pretty white teeth and clear complexion led me to believe her country life with fresh air and more food had given her an advantage over those of us from the city. She came from a large family, eight brothers and sisters.

One cold winter morning Krista and I walked into Chemnitz. I carried my accordion but my fingers were too cold to play. Most of the activity was, as usual, at the railroad station so we went there to see what was happening. People were sitting around on top of bundles and luggage, waiting for trains. The large restaurant was packed with people. Tables were spread with white tablecloths but no food or drinks; the serving counter was closed. A f e w soldiers were playing cards. The only sound seemed to be the shuffle and snap of cards as they were played. It was plain to see that people wore any kind of clothing they could get. Parts of military uniforms were worn with mismatched civilian apparel. A common sight was the gray military boots with worn out uniforms. A melancholy mood was everywhere.

Let's sing and I'll play, Krista."

We started. Heads turned and people smiled. This was the encouragement we needed. We sang some of the old German folk songs. "A penny and a Dollar," and "When all fountains are running" and others.

Coins were tossed toward us as we played and sang more. A young man picked up the coins and put them in his hat then gathered in more as they were tossed.

After a long while we stopped to rest. e spread the money on a the white tablecloth before us. I can still see it today. Happily we counted it and divided it between us.

"Krista, we could use this money to ride the trains Out to places where food is more plentiful."

An idea was born and we decided to try it. With permission from our mothers, who gave it only reluctantly, we traveled out toward Dresden, from there to Cottbus and into farmlands. We came home with kernels of wheat and occasionally some lard.

We travelled to Riesa and Meissen. Our singing and playing in railroad stations brought more coins. We used those coins for a travel and necessities.

When night came we slept in waiting rooms of rail road stations, hunched against the wall, or on a bench if one was empty. Sleeping in railroad stations had become a common way for everyone to travel, since no hotel rooms were available in bombed cities.

Police occasionally disturbed us when they came to check our IDs and tickets. Some German police overlooked our playing and singing, since it was clearly evident people seemed happier when they heard us. More often though, they forbade us to play in no uncertain terms, whether we had a ticket to travel or not. Anyone without a ticket had to leave the station and might even be arrested.

We were told, "You better watch out for the Russian patrol,""They won't allow any singing and playing in rail road stations" and they warned us that we could get arrested just for that.

Some young kids around the stations kept watch for us. When the Russian patrol approached they whistled a warning and we stopped and disappeared into the crowd.

The Russians usually checked identification papers at random. Sometimes they ordered us to open our bags to inspect the contents. They were always on the lookout for escaping Nazi officials or Ukrainians trying to get into West Germany. They arrested enough people that it made all of us afraid whenever they came through the door.

Since few women went out during evening hours or at night because of the danger of rape, my boy disguise gave me some protection and much greater freedom to move about. With Krista in the role as my sister she was not bothered by the Russians. We became skilled at bartering as we roamed the country side and the railroad stations looking for food. We traded some of the Meissen porcelain figurines that Grandma had given us for food. Of course the Meissen figurines were valuable antique, but hunger hurts. We bartered everything away.

At the more prosperous farmlands around Magdeburg we could get a piece of bacon or a tiny bottle of oil for a figurine. For a silver spoon I could sometimes get a small piece of butter or small sack of flour. We traveled to places where refugees had not come in such large numbers. Mama worried when I was gone but she was thankful for the food I brought home. Krista and I carefully divided our bartered items and broadened the area of our search.

One day while singing and playing in the waiting room at the Riesa railroad station, the Russian patrol came so quickly we could not escape. Shouting in Russian that we had committed a crime, they arrested us.

"We have been looking for you two a long time," said one of the patrol. "You have broken the law. No entertainment is allowed in rail road stations."

They yanked my accordion from me, forced us outside and into a truck. It was evening when they took us into the military police Headquarters. Searchlights were all over the building and a red star on top of it looked like a Christmas tree top. Their music was so loud we did not hear what they said, they just motioned us where to go. We were taken into a large room where an officer shouted orders in Russian we could not understand. The men who had arrested us were shouting and cursing. I could not see my accordion. One of them looked at us and shouted something. He paused as though waiting for an answer.

"Do you have my accordion?" I asked.

Apparently he did not understand me. I pantomimed what I meant and my question was answered in clumsy German. "I don't understand. "You broke the law and you will be punished," was what they repeated over and over. They took us out in the hail where we waited for about an hour with a soldier guarding us.

Suddenly a door burst open and two men shoved us back into the office where we had been. They took our ID cards, the contents of my pockets, and Krista's handbag. After looking at our things they dumped them in a box. They made fun of me of all the girl stuff I had in my pockets, I did not reveal myself and would not dare, since I always used my brother Ortwin's ID.

With nothing left but our clothing and I with my large felt boots, we were forced up a flight of stairs, through the building and downstairs again. They opened a door and pushed us down another flight of stairs into a hail below ground level. An iron door was unlocked revealing a dark room. After coming from the lighted rooms upstairs, the room looked totally black. They pushed us in and I stumbled and fell down a step I could not see. The door banged shut and someone helped me stand up. My hands were wet and we were standing in ankle deep water.

As my eyes adjusted to the darkness I could see we were in a room about 8 by 10 feet and it was full of people all standing close to one another. The cold water looked very dirty and the odor of urine grew stronger as my senses became more aware of our prison room. I shuddered to think I had touched the water and dried my hands on my clothes.

In the dim light I saw a well dressed couple next to us. The man looked like a black marketeer, because he did not look hungry. Krista grabbed my hand and whispered loudly, "They've put us in here until they kill us or send us to Siberia!"

"Don't be frightened," a calm voice said.

His soothing voice sounded inappropriate in this strange prison. Other people, mostly men, stood quietly sometimes speaking in low voices. I touched the wall. It was slippery and wet. Hours passed.

"How long can we stand this?" Krista asked. "My knees ache and my feet are numb."

I didn't answer. We held each other and cried quietly. Others sobbed and moaned.

"How long? How long?" I groaned. "I can't feel my legs anymore.

Hours later the couple still talked to each other ever so quietly. I was amazed at everyone's calmness. We counted the hours by the chimes of a church clock we could hear ever so faintly through our prison walls.

Many hours later we heard footsteps. Someone turned a key in a lock. The door opened and a man called out our names. I could not walk. I tried and fell against a man. They lifted us out but my legs still would not move. I dared not rub them for fear I'd fall back into that stinking hole. The Russian guards lfited us and dragged us up the steps and down a hall. They talked in Russian which we did not understand. When they let go of us we fell. By flexing the muscles in my legs the feeling gradually came back. We helped each other to a standing position.

We were taken through the same passage as the evening before and to the same office. A different officer was there now. With much gesturing he said, "You will be put away for good if you are caught in a railroad station again."

He said much more that we could not understand. When I saw our things I knew we were going to be released. I could not see my accordion and asked the officer for it. He questioned the patrolman. By their gestures I could see they told him they had not seen it.

"You didn't even have an accordion, you little liar," he bellowed. "If you don't shut up and get out of here we'll arrest you again and never let you go!"

We left quickly, anxious to be free of that awful prison. As

We hurried to catch the train, the cold wind penetrated our wet footwear. My boots weighted a ton. After hours of waiting we finally boarded the train to Chemnitz, but not without using our elbows fighting to get on since at the same time, hundreds of people wanted to get on the train as well. Being on the train even though standing all the way home, it felt very comfortable after the sleepless night standing in water.

BARTERING

As we arrived in Chemnitz, I said to Krista, "We're in pretty bad shape to go home." I looked down at my old wet boots. "They aren't much to look at anymore."

We were hungry. Our trip was a total loss and I had seen my accordion for the last time.

"I have some friends on Zschopauer Street. Let's go see if we can clean up there and rest before we start walking home."

Krista nodded her approval and we sloshed along in our wet footwear toward the Hillebrandt home. On the way I told Krista about this amazing family with 12 children.

"They have a coal business. It has been in their family for generations. When the coal comes in, the whole family helps to shovel it into heavy black sacks and in the good old days, deliver it to the customers. Since the war, people are lucky if they can pick just a halve sack up themselves. Right now, times are hard for the Hillebrand's too. That family always used to look black and grimy from their work but Mama used to say, 'that is black gold.' My parents knew them since before the war. They are really nice people."

"When I was smaller, I went there and they thought I belonged to them. When I hugged their Mama she said, 'Sit down baby and eat your soup.' Everybody was "baby" to her. I sometimes wonder if she remembers all their names. They all help take care of one another because Frau Hillebrandt works with her husband. They have six bedrooms and feed anyone who is there at mealtime."

When we arrived everyone started talking as though they had seen me the day before. Herr Hillebrandt said, "Go wash up you dirty little sparrow." His glance included Krista.

Their house was always kind of dark. Most of their windows faced a brick wall which seemed to take away all the daylight. Nevertheless, it was a place to live in this bombed out city.

I pulled Krista down the hail and we found the bathroom. After lighting a briquette in a little hot water stove we waited for the water to heat. After bathing we washed all our clothes with curd homemade soap and hung them to dry. In borrowed house robes, we joined the family activities which was grinding a sack of wheat kernels in a hand turned coffee mill. Since I offered to help they accepted me as one of their own.

We stayed overnight to let our clothes dry. Next morning, after a bowl of grounded wheat cooked in water and topped with Cinnamon and saccharin, we left and walked all the way to Euba.

With no accordion there was no way to make money and we had no articles to trade for food in the black market. A few days later, Mama made a visit to Zschopauer Strasse and to ask Herr Hillebrandt, carrying a large bag of rutabagas for that family, to make a trip to the Musik and Toy Towns Klingenthal and Zwothal. In order to find a new accordion for me. Krista and I joined her. Sure enough, he wanted to go with us. His oldest daughter Rosie, his friend Gustav Neumann, Krista, myself and Mr. Hillebrandt made up our group. We caught a train to Klingenthal, where we changed to a smaller train which took us to Zwothal. This train traveled a slowly because it

25

passed many pedestrian crossings and the engineer continually clanged its warning bell. Bim, bim, birn, bim," which gave the train it's name of "Bimrnelbahn."

From the windows of the Bimmelbahn we could see the spectacular mountains and lush green pine forests along the Erzgebirge. In Zwothal we walked to the factories where they made accordions other small instruments and wooden articles. "We are not making instruments for the German population, only for Russian needs," was the disheartening information we received.

Seeing my fallen expression, one of the workers in another factory thrust an accordion at me saying, "The Russians have a different musical scale. Here, try it. You cannot play it." I looked at an accordion smaller than the one taken from me and certainly not as attractive. I reached for the instrument and found it difficult to play. The notes didn't sound right. I thought of the Russian who would have to learn the scale on my accordion and wondered if he had thrown it away or really learned to play it.

Herr Hillebrandt had heard me play my old accordion. He looked at me, scratched the back of his head and asked, "You want it? Think you can learn to play this one?"

"I'll learn, no matter what." I promised.

"Okay. You got it. He turned to the factory representative and said. "Sell it to me. The Russians took her accordion."

He peeled some money of f a roll he carried and with a wink at the factory people I now owned a new accordion. I put it in its brand new case and said a silent prayer of thanks to God. It was not as shiny as the first one but it was a nice instrument and brand new.

We stopped at all the little factories where tiny hand carved and painted figurines were made. They were so beautiful painted with much bright color, it felt as if we were visiting Santa Claus's workshop. We needed these items for trade on the black market. Russians who traded on the black market liked these figurines to. One shopkeeper refused to sell us anything and said, "These are all for the Russians and we have to account for everything." We knew these wooden carvings and parts for larger items, were made in the homes of village people who had been carvers for generations. We explained our need for small items so that we could trade them for food.

"Some of these items were brought in today and we could let you buy some of them. The carvers will be glad for some extra business."

Once again persuasion had worked and we were able to buy some wooden carved items. On the train going home I gave Herr Hillebrandt other addresses where he might get food in exchange for the carvings he bought. After all, he had a very large family to feed.

After many days of practice I was ready to play my new accordion. Since Krista and I did not always have money to buy train tickets, we traveled in empty boxcars on freight trains as many other Germans traveled. People who were looking for lost relatives mostly traveled by boxcar.

Sympathetic railroad employees allowed people to ride in the empty boxcars. Upon catching someone riding the freight train illegally, the kinder employee would ask the rider to get off at the next stop. Railroad authorities took no responsibility for the safety of free riders and not all railroad workers showed sympathy.

Russian patrols were greatly feared by everyone. They were everywhere, swaggering about with machine guns strapped to their bodies. The government occasionally used the boxcars to transport large amounts of refugees. When this happened, there was usually a full transport, organized and handled by authorities. Refugees were still coming out like that from (Silesia, East Prussia) Poland S and (Sudetenland) Czechoslovakia.

It was in this kind of situation that Krista and I first learned to catch free rides, using the uncomfortable boxcars. We soon learned how to appeal to the sympathetic ear of the railroad worker. When caught, we were "just a couple of kids, lost," or "trying to find my Papa." Using these sob-stories, we talked our way past the police and railway employees. We learned how to stand along the railroad tracks in hopes of learning where the train was going yet not appear to want a ride. Because of undetermined time schedules, we never boarded until the train started to move. Then would run and jump into a boxcar.

One morning Krista and I caught a freight train going north to Leipzig. From Leipzig we changed to another freight train going on to Halle, about twenty miles further north. Halle lay in ruins.

Once thousands of people lived in this city. Many have moved away and also a large number of people have perished. We did not see many of the population that day. The chemical plants and food industries built along the Saale river were totally destroyed and most of the rail yards lay in tangled wreckage. I felt the wasteful defeat our country was suffering all because of Hitler.

"Koethen is almost straight north," Krista said. "Should we try it?"

"Let's go." I said. We shouldered our knapsacks and boarded the next train heading north. Koethen was damaged by bombs but not like

28

the city of Halle. We made our way out to a farm area and bartered our tiny figurines for oat kernels, a small sack of flour, some barley and a 4 oz. bottle of beechnut oil. Beechnut oil was made from the Beechtree fruit. Tiny little nut like fruit, which we called "Bucheckers". In late fall, they told us, pick your own "Bucheckers" if you want oil. So we spend many hours to pick up those little kernels to have enough for just a tiny bottle oil.

Our load was heavy for two skinny kids and we stopped many times to rest as we returned to the railroad station. We soon caught a freight train back to Halle. We jumped off in Halle only to find the station filled with people. Another train had just rolled in but it was so full that people were hanging on the steps of the railroad cars and outside the doors. There were soldiers in tattered uniforms were sitting on top of the train. I wondered if Papa would come home this way.

We learned that Russia was demanding restitution from Germany. The one who loses a war always must pay to the winners. However, Russia wanted more than what Germany had ever been worth. We saw railroad tracks removed by German POWs and shipped to Russia along with just about anything else that was of value. From a clothing factory every single sewing machine was send to Russia. By losing so much railroad tracks, now we had such a crippled train system it was no wonder people were so excited about the arrival of two trains at once.

We stood at the place where people boarded trains even as we watched we knew we would not be able to get on this train with our bags of food. It was just too crowded. We plunked down to rest and to wait in front of two low basement windows.

"Look Krista, we can see down into the kitchen of the restaurant. I wonder for whom they are cooking?" Hungrily we sniffed the kitchen smells. The cook saw us and smiled. We waved back then turned to watch for the next train.

A tap on the window caused us to turn and back around and saw the cook gesturing for us to come in. "You kids out there. Come into the kitchen and I'll give you a bowl of soup."

He didn't have to repeat this offer. We quickly gathered up our bags and found the stairway down to the kitchen.

The aroma of food brought tears to my eyes. I'll never forget how good that warm soup felt in my stomach.

"You kids look kind of undernourished. Here, have a piece of bread."

Greatful for his kindness, we devoured the soup and bread. That meal was one of the best I have ever eaten. The cook asked us where we came from and told me to take my hat off. When I didn't, he took it off for me, His eyes opened wide. a

"What kind of a boy are you?" For an instant he was not sure if I was a boy or a girl.

Slapping me on the back he said, "Break your neck and a leg." Which is an old German saying for wishing someone luck. I think he decided not to give my disguise away. A sudden commotion outside caught our attention. The cook and other people in the kitchen ran to the high basement windows to see what was happening. We heard people running. Krista and I scrambled up on a chair next to the cook to look outside. A train had just pulled in. People were sitting on the rooftops and hanging on doors and windows. Only a few people got off and at least a hundred tried to get on. People were trying to get on from both sides of the tracks. They were pushing one another and shouting.

Then to our surprise we saw two nuns in their black robes screaming and running away from the train over the tracks toward the main station. Several Russian soldiers were in full pursuit and apparently very intoxicated. The nuns were trying to reach the station building where they thought they would find safety.

No one dared to stop the Russians in their drunken state. People were forced to watch as they knocked the nuns to the ground and raped them. Bottles of vodka stuck out of the pockets of the Russians overcoats. Those who saw it, clenched their jaws in anger, then hung their heads in despair.

"I'll kill them!" cried the cook, grabbing a large butcher knife and starting for the door. Quickly his two helpers restrained him and said, "We lost the war. We have to put up with these acts of violence."

"Not to nuns!" The cook sat down and put his head in his hands and cursed. We finished our meal and thanked the cook. "You kids be careful getting that food home to your folks," he warned.

Touching my shoulder, the cook whispered, "Survive, little buddy. It's better for now, to be a boy."

I pulled my hat on and we left. "We've got to get on that train for Leipzig in order to get home. We worked our way across the tracks, then pushed and squeezed ourselves into one of the cars.

"I'm glad we have train tickets to get home this time," Krista said as we squeezed into an aisle and sat on our bags of food. There was a heavy scent of soap in the air. Several people were probably carrying large amounts of it. This would make it hard for us since the police

31

would be more likely to inspect our bags and take our food. The authorities called us hamsterers (hoarders). Police had forbidden people to barter for food. Farmers, busy with the harvest and other farm chores, grew impatient with hungry people coming to their doors. They became overloaded with silver, crystal, oriental rugs and fur coats. In one village, the state farms had hung out a sign saying, "No bartering. We have everything we need except an oriental rug in the cow barn."

Arriving in Leipzig we learned the next train to Chemnitz would leave early next morning. We slept on the floor of the station waiting room to catch the early train for Chemnitz and then on to Niederwiesa.

Krista sniffed the air. "This car smells of coffee." We tucked our bags of food down as tight as possible and I put my accordion on top.

Loud talking at the other end off the car alerted us to Russian patrols with two German police officers acting as interpreters. As they began checking ID's and tickets, hands moved rapidly to conceal belongings and have IDs ready.

The Russians held their noses high in the air looking at the overhead luggage. As they neared us, we could tell they smelled the coffee.

"Who is the one with the coffee?" an officer demanded. "This woman has the coffee," said a man pointing to the woman next to him.

"I have only a little more than a pound," she protested.

They took it from her. No amount of begging or crying helped.

They moved on through the car, deaf to her pleading. Fellow travelers expressed anger and disgust at the informer. The woman scolded and cursed him.

When the patrol left the car, the man said to her, "Calm down lady I have a whole knapsack full of the stuff. I diverted them to you so I could keep mine." He reached into his bag and gave the lady the amount she had just lost. People smiled and held on tight to their bags.

In Chemnitz we changed trains to Niederwiesa and were soon carrying our heavy bags of food home to Euba.

On another day Krista and I caught a freight train north, planning to go to Riesa. My accordion was strapped to my back and a sack of tobacco from our garden was fastened in front. Somehow we ended up going in the wrong direction. For hours we did not know where we were.

When we realized our mistake, we didn't dared to jump off the moving train. A train man found us when he came to check the boxcars. "What are a couple of kids like you doing on the train?"

"We are looking for our folks," I ventured.

"Where are we?" Krista asked.

"This train is going east. You are east of Finsterwalde, going toward the border of Poland."

"We were trying to get to Riesa," I said.

"You are on the wrong train for sure. I'll see what I can do at the next stop." With that he left us.

We weren't sure if he would help us or turn us in to the police. After a while we decided to believe him and stayed on the train. He returned just as the train slowed for the next station and pointed to another freighter.

"See if you can get on that one, but don't get caught. Run!" We jumped off the slower moving train, ran across the tracks to a freight train going in the opposite direction, and scrambled into a boxcar. Greatly relieved, we relaxed. I played my accordion and other free-riders, hiding in the boxcar, sang along with us. The war had scattered people all around and a big migration was in progress. The train had to be side-tracked so often for other trains we slept the night in the boxcar.

Early the next morning we saw the sign "Riesa" and got ready to jump off. Most of the others stayed on and we waved to them as they rolled on toward Dresden. The first thing we looked for in the station was the washroom. We needed to clean ourselves up and tidy our clothes as best as we could.

"Riesa has a black market, we just have to find it." I said as we walked toward the main street.

We had heard the Russians would trade food for good tobacco. Their government allowance of tobacco (Russian Machorka) was a coarse stinking stuff. Machorka is one of the coarsest Russian tobacco there is. Machorka is not made out of tobacco leaves, but out of the stems. Those stems are cut very small almost like sawdust, That is how it tasted to. Then the Russian soldier rolled the stuff into a small piece of newspaper and this was what they smoked. Surely, they would like our tobacco better. As we approached a coffeehouse, we saw the large sign advertising movies across the Street. It was midmorning and we were hungry. Few restaurants had food to serve and when they did the customer had to bring some of the ingredients.

34

For example, three potatoes bought you a bowl of potato soup, etc. Most people did not even have a burner to boil their potatoes. So, the arrangement to bring produce to the restaurant in exchange for meals was ideal. However, patrons also had to pay a nominal charge for the service. A few customers were already inside and the owner was busy behind the counter.

"Do you have food?" I asked. "We have tobacco." I took some from my sack and his expression told me he was interested.

"You kids sit down, I'll fix you both a breakfast."

He served us a cup of chicory, a bowl of hot cereal and a L slice of bread with plum preserves. "A breakfast fit for a king,"

I said. We figured he must have a connection with some farm for his food supplies.

"Do you know the Russian guards? Do you think they would trade food for tobacco?" Krista asked.

"The Russian guards are across the street. They have that dance hail connected to the movie house and it's full of German POWs. They're waiting to be shipped to Russia. The guards won't come over here until after lunch. Wait here if you wish."

We decided to wait. We considered going down to the Elbe River to see what was left of the steel mills. We had been told the bomb damage was extensive and many of the 37,000 people who had lived there must have been killed or moved to other places.

Shortly after noon we heard the guards coming. I was scared but tried to hide it. They were laughing and talking. Seeing Krista, they approached us but I eluded their attention in my boy's disguise. I felt uneasy that they might try something with Krista and hoped the presence of the bartender would protect us. They were friendly and spoke a few German words. Krista had a quick answer for everything, causing them to laugh. Then I got down to business acting as her "brother." I put some tobacco between my fingers and held it out to them. I put enough tobacco on the table to roll two cigarettes. Our cigarette papers, bought on the black market in Chemnitz, were the finest. The Russians usually rolled their coarse tobacco in newspaper which makes it stink. They looked at me then at Krista then they inspected the tobacco.

"Smells good, Karoscho. Where more?" He eyed my knapsack.

"We don't have it with us but we can get it." We used our hands to make ourselves understood.

"We want food. No money, food only."

They talked among themselves then left, indicating they would return. Sure enough, they came back and we exchanged our tobacco for commisbread, a small sack of flour, and 8 ounces of bacon. We were pleased. The bacon alone would have cost the whole bag of tobacco on the black market in Chemnitz.

"Krista, We must go now." I said nervously.

"Stay and go to the movies with us," invited the coffeehouse owner. "Several of us are going."

It was very tempting as I had not seen a movie for a very long time. So, with our food locked safely in the icebox, we went to the movies. The movie house was full of young German POWS. Their uniforms looked clean compared to the shabby tunic tops over britches and boots worn by the Russian guards.

While we waited for the film to start, one of the Russian guards took of f his boot. He unwound a large cloth from his foot, then rewrapped his foot and pulled his boot back on again.

36

Amazed, I nudged Krista, "He has no socks, only rags wound around his feet."

"Do you suppose all of them are without real socks?" Krista whispered.

"I don't know but I suspect so."

We sat with the owners of the coffee house while the Russian guards sat in front and behind of us. We continued, waiting for the movie to start but nothing happened. Nothing but silence; Minutes ticked by still no picture.

Krista whispered, "Play and we'll sing to them." She pushed me up and I got my accordion out of the case. We walked into the aisle and we began to sing. We started with the popular songs, then played:

Yes you men oh you men

you are all heartbreaker's

we know your heart's are a dark hole.

The entire male audience replied as with one strong masculine voice:

But the women are not any better

still, lovely, oh so lovely

they are nevertheless.

Their voices rang with a thunderous rhythmic sound . We led them in another song, " A Penny and a Dollar."

A penny and a dollar

they were both mine, yes mine.

The penny bought me water

the dollar bought me wine, yes wine

The penny bought me water, but the dollar

bought me wine. Hydee hy do hy da,

37

by de hy do hy da, hy dee, hy do, hy da....

This powerful melody and their rich voices swept the air with a heart stirring sound, vibrating the whole movie house. Fearful that we might start something, the Russian signaled frantically for the lights to be turned out and the movie to start. The movie started and everyone became silent again.

After the movie ended we got our food from the icebox, paid a strip of bacon for our breakfast, and went to the railroad station where we bought train tickets home. As ususal we walked from the station home under the cover of darkness. Food was of great value and we were safer carrying it during darkness. The police always confiscated everything when they caught "hoarders" they called us.

Krista and I divided our food and she walked quietly of f into the night. I threw little stones at our window to signal Mama. She peered through the window, then came down to unlock the door.

Each time I returned the boys would lift their sleepy heads and ask for food. It was hard to sleep soundly when we were so hungry. While Mama cooked us a meal, I heated water in the washhouse downstairs, using a few sticks of wood. I took a bath in the zinc tub in the middle of the night. Upstairs again, we talked a long time about my trip. The boys were always anxious to hear about my adventures.

"I don't know where you get your courage, girl."

"From you Mama. You are my rock. You are able to keep us all together while others are dying of starvation."

"You are keeping us alive, Irene."

After a meal of commisbread, bacon and chicory we all slept without hunger pains that night.

Ration cards became almost worthless but still they were given out. At the store it was the same old story. "We are out of everything but save your ration cards. Perhaps we will have something for sale next week." But they never did.

We continued our early morning task of picking nettle leaves which grew in abundance. While everyone slept, Mama was out picking Stinging nettle, a weed difficult to get rid of, grew until heavy frost in November. Mama would serve each of us a bowl of spinach-like soup with one potato swimming in it. This was often all the food we had in one day. Word got around that a pig was being butchered and every person would get rationed 2 ounces. This meant our family would get 12 ounces. We stood in line, four abreast for hours, waiting for our portion. The butchers sliced the Meat paper thin when our turn to buy came around we got only four strips.

Winter arrived long and dreary. Grandmother, now 76 years old, often walked eleven miles through the snow to get food from us. Many times she walked back home with only a few potatoes and sugar beets in her net bag. She came one day in February, Grandpa had walked in another direction to look for food. Mama gave her some of the food brought home from my black market trading.

Extremely tired from her trip, when she came home from us. Grandmother put some potatoes to boil on their gas stove, then fell asleep. The potatoes boiled over and extinguished the flame. The gas poured out and my Grandmother never awakened. Our sorrow was magnified since we wished that one of us had walked home with her. Grandpa loved her dearly and died ten days later. He just gave up living.

We inherited a few of Grandmother's things, her Meissen china, some blankets, featherbeds and a chandelier with teardrop crystals. One of Papas's sisters came also and took alot of furniture away. Mama received a notification from the Chemnitzer Registration Office (Einwohnermeldeamt.) that we could move into Grandmother's apartment which needed much repair. However, there was a new restriction that people must help in building up the city from the rubble in order to get worthless ration cards. Since working in the ruins paid such a meager wage and would buy even more meager food, Mama decided we should stay in the village. Food was easier to find there.

Krista and I continued our search for food. One day we went north to Leipzig. We planned to go on to Dessau but we were caught in a police raid. The raid took place in a partially destroyed railroad station. They crowded about a hundred of us into the police station which was located inside the station building.

Children were arrested since they were considered as cunning as adults in the black market trade and every bit as hungry. Sometimes a child could run away, but not today. The police saw my bag and I knew they suspected I was carrying forbidden items. Our knapsack held only a few items which we had planned to use for trading, I did however have a pile of sanitary napkins which I needed. Suddenly I remembered my bar of American Life Buoy soap. I had bought it on the black market in Chemnitz and I considered it a hot item. Now it was a dangerous piece of evidence for which I could expect a good several years in jail. I slipped the soap out of my bag and held it up my sleeve while looking for a place to discard it. As the police pushed us along in the line, I saw a crevice in the cracked wall. I threw it deep in the opening. If no one saw it I would retrieve it later.

At the police station, we were summoned to a desk where our names were recorded. They lined us up, men and boys on one side of the room, girls and women on the other. I stayed on the girl's side even though I was disguised as a boy. I was called to the officer's desk first. "What's in your bag?" he demanded.

I hugged it and replied, "Not much."

He stood up. "Come here!" he ordered. He grabbed my bag and dumped the contents on the desk, all my sanitary napkins- -

People began to laugh. He was embarrassed.

"What are you, a boy, doing with such things?"

He checked my name and realized I was a girl. Frustrated and angry, he ripped of f my cap. He seemed speechless. Finally he blustered, "Put your stuff together!"

He tore up the paper with my name on and threw it in the wastebasket. People hid their smiles but worried for themselves because on such raids there were always arrests made.

"Out you go and don't you ever let me see you again," he bellowed as his face turned beet red.

I left quickly. While waiting for Krista I looked for my soap. It was gone. I looked at the people around me and was pretty sure who had taken it by the expression on his face. I dared not say anything, since that bar of soap was risky to possess if searched. I hoped the new owner would have difficulty when they searched him. We left Leipzig on a freight car going north. After that experience I was not fond of the city of Leipzig.

Rumors still came to us that Papa might be alive where he had been seen I could not find him. I always combined my search for Papa with my search for food. It was a convenient excuse when queried by authorities, especially when I was a long distance from home.

We heard Papa might be in West Germany. If he had been at our old home and saw nothing but rubble he might have moved on, thinking we were all dead. The notice we had left to tell anyone our new address, must surely have been long washed Out by the rain by now.

"Mama, do you think Papa could be in West Germany?"

"If he thought we all died in the air raid, there would be nothing to keep him here, he might had moved on with the others, to West Germany." She got out an old map and we studied it, trying to figure out where the trains traveled near the border.

"It would be dangerous child, but perhaps he is there."

When I saw the hope in Mama's face I felt compelled to extend my search into West Germany.

Krista's parents would not allow her to go. This time I was on my own. Since people could be shot on sight in the border area, I would have to be very careful. Mama and I decided it would be best not to tell anyone except Ortwin about this trip.

It was too risky to even tell Hartmut and Claus.

I did not take as much with me as I had on other excursions, no accordion and no items for bartering. I wore the only clothes I had, the black SS pants, shirt, coat and the oversized boots.

With a short hair cut and my motorcycle cap I looked like a boy. In my knapsack I packed a spoon, a change of underclothing, a comb and a small piece of homemade soap in a towel. With Ortwin's ID card buttoned securely in my breast pocket I was ready to take on the world.

"Just in case you get hungry take these." Mama held out two raw carrots. I put them in my knapsack, wondering where she had got them from.

"God go with you." As I left, tears were in her eyes but I knew her hope of finding Papa was constant.

BORDER CROSSING

Early in March of 1947 I set out to find my way across the border from East into West Germany. It was a cold wintery day. Snow still covered the ground and an icy wind was blowing. I had a few marks in my pocket intended for train tickets in the event I could not find a ride in a boxcar. From my hometown Chemnitz I was able to catch one to the next town Glauchau. No freight train was to be found that went from there to the next town of Zwickau that day, so I bought a ticket and rode the passenger train. As I arrived in Zwickau I found that I had to change trains if I want to travel farther south.

This railroad station was very busy, although smaller than the one in Chemnitz. Here, people rode the train to go to work at the uranium mines, and they waited around occupying every available seat in the waiting area. I was now in a restricted area. ID's were checked constantly by Russian and German soldiers; I felt, I better avoid them. I had only my brother's ID and I had no explanation why I traveled through a restricted area. I did not want to get arrested as a spy. They would not believe any other explanation. It was an uranium mining district from here on, way up to the silver Erzgebirge, mountains with historical value. Once there was active mining for silver and other minerals. People who lived in those beautiful pine tree covered mountains were artistic woodcarvers. The famous Nutcracker was created here and many other charming delightful wooden figurines.

Now the Russian-German WISMUT Corporation mined uranium. Workers were working with no protection from radiation; eventually they would all be sick or worse. Still, people fought to get those jobs, for the pay was good and WISMEJT ration cards were honored in food stores. Food was more important than money. This railroad station was very busy, although smaller than the one in Chemnitz. But here, people rode the train to go to work into the uranium mines and they walked around in their large miner's boots and garb. The MP's stopped mostly travelers who did not look like miners, so I knew I better spend my time waiting for the next train somewhere else.

As I walked down the main Street my eye caught sight of a neighborhood pub. It was closed, but people were inside, cleaning and preparing for the evening business. I must have looked like so many of those homeless pitiful children who have come from the Silesia, and East and West Prussia territory, (now Poland), in search of their parents or any family members.

They had pity on me, and knowing that I must have been hungry, gave me a cup of hot water that smelled like bouillon to which I added my two raw carrots Mama had given me for my trip. I heard one of the cleaning women saying, "This little boy sure looks like he has come a long way". "Poland?" suggested the other. I thanked them with a smile and stayed quiet in my corner where they seated me until I had to go back to the railroad station.

The next train took me to Plauen. A once very charming small town, parts of it were in ruins from the war. Again I bought a ticket on a passenger train since I had a definite destination. Two men in western clothing waiting on the platform, I suspected, by their speech, were Czechoslovakians and must have been on the other side of the border before. A trail of ragged people, men and women, followed the two men, who tried desperately to lose them. Instead, more people hung on their trail. Of course, instinctively we knew that those two men knew the way across the border and that was where we wanted to go but we didn't know the way.

As we followed them we had to catch a train quickly, no matter how overcrowded, and by not leaving the embankment we were able to change trains many times. We struggled on and off trains and those two men were always shouting, "Stand back". But I knew I had to follow them or never make it over the border. It was an exhausting maneuver until only the boldest and strongest were still with us. After all that zigzag riding we came back to Plauen and here we regrouped. Now the two Czechoslovakian men decided it was easier to take the rest of us over the border instead run around and draw attention from the border patrol. They were everywhere. Plauen was a dreary place. The railroad station had been almost completely destroyed. A wooden shack took its place which was full of people and the stench of putrid air took me ten paces back.

I'd rather freeze out here then wait inside I thought. But when I saw them putting their heads together I had to hear what was going on; I didn't want to be left behind. Just when I decided to go in, a Russian and German patrol drove up in an old, open truck. Somebody inside gave a signal and I heard many of the people scramble out of the back entrance. I sensed we must be close to the border but I didn't know exactly where to turn. At this time and place, it was better not to have a map on one's person. If caught by the patrol it could be deadly.

Ragged people of all ages were standing around the embankment waiting for a train to take them somewhere. It was getting dark now and our group was still together. After catching another train which traveled away from Plauen we had by nightfall worked ourselves closer to the border. Even though it was cold, I got warm from running, hiding, jumping, and just keeping up with the two leaders.

We finally reached the last train station, beyond was no man's Land. Several miles of land in between borders where no human other than patrols were allowed to be. So we had to start walking. The leaders counted 22 people, among us there were German soldiers who ran away from the Russians and wanted to rather be a POW with the Americans than the Bolsheviks. Some had come all the way by foot from the Balkan States and Prussia, always a small step ahead from the Red Army. The Red Army of course would have made them POW's and Siberia would be their destiny. They knew Stalin had no mercy. Some women were among us but no children.

Everyone carried something, but most of us traveled light and we all were very hungry. We had apparently gone as far southwest as possible by train. Now we marched through small villages. It was dark and people had closed their curtains. No light escaped to the outside, a total blackout, as if the war was still on. We walked exhausted and soundlessly until we reached the little town of Lobenstein.

One person among us whispered, "The only light seen here is from Russian Patrol Stations."

"Quiet!" sharply whispered one of the Czechoslovakians. "No talking or else." He made an intimidating gesture.

The roads were still snow covered and icy and although a cold wind pushed us forward, I was hot and my feet felt like a ton with those greatly oversized large felt boots I wore on my feet. These were the kind of boots that we had found at the uniform factory just before the war ended. The only footwear I owned since we lost everything in the war. Almost at the end of the main street in Lobenstein we came to an iron gate. Beyond the gate we saw the contours of a medium building in complete darkness.

"Hurry it up," whispered a male voice as we passed through the gate and continued silently toward the building. As we reached the entrance someone gave the signal to halt.

"Once we are in, it is vital that you don't talk to anyone. Eat the food they give you and keep quiet. We are sure that there are informers around."

As we nodded in agreement, the door was pushed open and the smell of food reached us. It was a heavenly smell.

Only a small group of 6 at a time were able to go into a sort of vestibule which was pitch dark. Then, as the outside door was closed, another door was opened which lead into a spacious dining room. The sudden light and the warm air was a welcome sight. The warmth made my face and hands tingle. It was a village pub and the smoke-filled room revealed all sorts of shabby people; many local, but most of them strangers. There were several tables that seated four to six people I found a chair and put my bags beside it.

Over the kitchen window I saw a sign which read, " Noodle soup 35 Pfennige." While some people went to get something to drink, I went to get a plate of soup. Although there were no spoons, I fished one out of my bag. I had not seen such a rich noodle soup for a very long time, it even had meat in it. While I ate I became drowsy and I could hardly keep my eyes open. One of the soldiers in a torn uniform sat at my table, he kept saying, "Eat up, boy. Eat up.TM He meant me. I still wore my fabric Lindberg-type cap which had moved down over my forehead and it almost covered my eyes. There was no reason for me to take it off, if I didn't want to be discovered as a girl. I thought, "If I could only close my eyes and sleep. Nothing else matters anymore. Just let me sleep, please..."

Just then I was pushed in the ribs and I picked up my bags along with the others. It was time to go. I saw some people arguing. Some woman had talked to a stranger and now the leaders of our group did not want to have anything to do with her. They wanted her to stay behind. We were told to move out into the dark room aiid then out into the street. The cold air woke me up some. As our group gathered silently our eyes adjusted to the dark. The leaders had come out too and the woman. As we got in a line, single file, our silhouettes were like black shadows in the snow. It was then that I heard a sound that reminded me of someone chopping wood. No one said so, but I knew, that woman who had not obeyed orders was not with us anymore. That quickly made me wide awake. We moved faster and our breathing was labored as we stepped carefully, since sound travels a long distance in the cold winter air. Silently and swiftly we moved along. The food had strengthened us and we increased our pace. I began to doubt my strength to keep up.

We were told that anyone dropping out would give the others away. I knew they had knives under their jackets and might kill anyone that got in their way. I shuddered when I thought of the woman at the pub. The situation was harsh; one person's weakness must not endanger the others. Our two leaders were determined to make it with or without us. We did not know them and we did not know each other. After millions had died in the war, the death of one person more or less wouldn't make a bit of difference.

49

We walked on level ground for a while and I found it easier. The path turned uphill again but we still moved at such a fast pace, that I gasped for breath. I wished now that I had stayed behind. I fell. I got up, and then fell again. I saw the distance between the last person and myself grow bigger yet I knew I must keep going.

The soldier with a small bundle over his shoulder looked back and saw me struggling. Without a word, he grabbed my hand and pulled me a few meters uphill. But it must have been a strain on him too, as he let go and I again began falling behind. Those oversized boots I was wearing seemed like heavy weights on my feet. For a while I crawled on all fours; the perspiration frozen on my hair and face.

"Come on!" the man motioned. I lurched forward until I was able to regain my stride. Finally, we made it to the top.

The leaders stopped for a few seconds to get orientated. This brief rest made me feel that I could keep up. The beautiful night scenery was all around us. The woods, pitch dark ahead of us, and fields , glistening silver white in the moonlight. Somewhere dogs were barking in the distance. We could only guess what lay ahead of us as we fearfully entered the dark woods.

Our leaders whispered, "Don't talk. Sound travels. Don't step on any wood. It will snap and give us away."

My heart was pounding so loud that I felt everyone around me could hear it. As we walked for several hundred meters through a forest aisle it lead us downhill and I heard running water. We fought our way through a thick brushy area until we saw a small river below us. The snow was deeper here. It must have snowed again the day before. The water was running so rapidly only the edges were snow covered. The stream was a good eight feet wide and too far to jump to the other side.

"Take off your boots. Shoulder them and cross!" was the whispered command. It had to be done in a hurry, the first ones were already in the water. One woman put her bare foot in the icy water and gave a shriek. The men with her hissed angrily. The soldier and I were just behind the Czechoslovakians. They saw how frail and tired I was.

"Look," one of them whispered in my ear. Over this mountain in front of us, there is freedom. Let's go and don't stay behind!" I cried silently, I knew not to show weakness. I prayed silently. As I prayed, I felt renewed energy return. The icy water was not the worst of it. It was all the sharp stones on the bottom that made it hard to walk through. If I don't make it, they will kill me here on the border. It happens every day and Mama and my brothers would wait in vain for my return. I had to get through that stream and up the hill again. The water reached up to my calves and I stepped carefully so as not to fall. As I wobbled up the slippery bank on the other side, my feet were numb. I looked down in the snow to see if my feet were still there. Silently, we pulled on our socks and boots and, when ready, started to walk slowly and close together. A dark human wall swaying back and forth as we silently climbed up the steep hill. My knees hurt as I lifted my heavy boots. The feeling was coming back into my feet.

Suddenly one of the women broke away from the group and ran recklessly downhill. She crashed into some bushes, snapping branches and knocking rocks loose. I thought the strain must have been too great for her or perhaps she lost something valuable where we waded through the stream. In that instant if it had been possible I knew the men would have killed her.

They cursed under their breath and urged us to run. "Faster! Faster!" Our dark figures could easily be seen in the snow.

By now border guards had heard us. We looked down as they ran along the river bank, shouting at us. "STOYI STOY!" (stop! stop!" and "STO TO KOY?" (What is going on?) They were shooting up into the air.

The first guard running toward us from the underbrush had his machine gun aimed straight at us. We raised our arms high and stood still. My heart roared and my pulse pounded in my head.

They too, were excited, not knowing whether we carried guns or how many we were. A guard's gun went off, snapping a limb from a tree. I saw the holes in the snow where the bullets landed. More Russian soldiers came and they swarmed all around us, thrusting their guns against our backs.

"DAWEY! DAWEY! DAWEY!" (Hurry! Hurry! Hurry!) . We were marched about a half mile along the river to a narrow bridge which we had to cross single file. There was a wooden blockhouse, which served as a check point for the border guards. We were pushed into the house and our eyes squinted in the bright lights. Russian soldiers, all over the place. Some who were lying around, sat up and put on their boots. I stared at their feet, they folded rags around them before they put their boots on. They had no socks.

The two Czechoslovakians motioned for us to keep quiet. They would do the talking. We finally were allowed to take our arms down and to find something to sit on. Our two leaders went to the guard in charge and talked loudly in a Slavic language. It could not be perfect

Russian but it was a heated argument. The shouting got real loud but only our group paid attention to it. The rest of the Russians were telling us to put our bags down and wait.

The raggedy German soldier finally thought he understood enough. Our two leaders tried to convince the Russians that we were trying to get from West Germany to East Germany. What a plot! Our Czechoslovakians were indeed clever fellows.

A Russian who spoke better German came in. He joined the heated debate and then said to the rest of us, "This is not possible. You must have permission. You cannot go over the border to visit relatives in the Russian Zone without it.

"Why, is it not Germany too?"

"You must go the legal way. Now you have broken the law. You all must wait until morning for the officer in charge. Then we will see." He said something to another guard and walked out of the room.

Morning was still several hours away and the warmth of the room made me drowsy. I looked around. We were in a large room with a potbelly stove right in the center. Around the stove were a few tables with hand irtade wooden benches. Along the walls double bunk beds were lined up. This is where the soldiers slept when they were of f duty. I was sure this building must have some more rooms in the back, which I could not see. Most people from our group sat at the tables, others sat right on the floor leaning against the bunk beds.

I took my heavy boots off and rubbed my cold feet. I saw others doing the same. Some people hung wet clothes around the potbelly stove. Our leaders took them down. Saying, "Do you want them to think we crossed the river?"

I sat on a bench and cradled my head in my arms at the table. I tried to sleep, but stirred occasionally as the men walked around in heavy boots. They seemed to be talking all the time.

Some of the soldiers tried to talk to the women, motioning for them to go outside. Some younger ones even flirted. I guess to some women, men are men no matter what. I was glad to be looked at as a boy. I felt warm and safe. I dozed uneasily for several hours.

The guards changed at dawn. Everyone awoke and stood as the new officer in charge came in and looked around. He walked to a table covered with papers and read the report.

I'll get a truck and transport all of them into town for interrogation," he said, We were frightened when we heard the translation.

What if they ask for ID'S, and they will. I only had a paper with my brother's name on it. They will search us and then I will be in real trouble.

The two Czechoslovakians approached the officer and protested. He must have called them every name in the book, I heard some cursing and everyone who lived in the Russian Zone understood what they meant. Back and forth they argued. Until the Russian officer became very angry. He wanted every man in a German uniform on one side of the room and the civilians and women on the other side. Those raggedy German soldiers were transported to the next town and we had no idea what became of them. As for us, we quickly

them to think we crossed the river?"

I sat on a bench and cradled my head in my arms at the table. I tried to sleep, but stirred occasionally as the men walked around in heavy boots. They seemed to be talking all the time.

Some of the soldiers tried to talk to the women, motioning for them to go outside. Some younger ones even flirted. I guess to some women, men are men no matter what. I was glad to be looked at as a boy. I felt warm and safe. I dozed uneasily for several hours.

The guards changed at dawn. Everyone awoke and stood as the new officer in charge came in and looked around. He walked to a table covered with papers and read the report.

I'll get a truck and transport all of them into town for interrogation," he said, We were frightened when we heard the translation.

What if they ask for ID'S, and they will. I only had a paper with my brother's name on it. They will search us and then I will be in real trouble.

The two Czechoslovakians approached the officer and protested. He must have called them every name in the book, I heard some cursing and everyone who lived in the Russian Zone understood what they meant. Back and forth they argued. Until the Russian officer became very angry. He wanted every man in a German uniform on one side of the room and the civilians and women on the other side. Those raggedy German soldiers were transported to the next town and we had no idea what became of them. As for us, we quickly gathered our things and started to leave.

"DAWEY! DAWEY! DAWEY! he yelled. (Hurry! Hurry! Hurry!)

Once out of the blockhouse, we were to go back where we came from.

After the hours of rest we'd had we felt stronger. we crossed the I bridge in a hurry and started to climb the hill. It looked to be a about

55

half a mile to the top. The ground was still snow covered but the morning winter sun was trying to thaw the snow and so it a was very slippery. There were still heavy batches of ice.

About one third the way up, we heard shouting again, "DAWEY! DAWEY!".

Then we heard shots. Maybe they regretted letting us go. We a climbed faster, fearful of being killed. My chest ached and my a legs hurt as I increased my speed. Bullets were hitting the rocks and ground all around us. a My knapsack felt like a ton. Then I heard a "bang," One of the a bullets had hit something inside my knapsack. Whatever it was, it had saved my life. I We saw people at the top of the hill and they were shouting.

Were we running into another police trap?

"Dear God, I can't take anymore of this!" I screamed.

"They're the Red Cross people on the western side!" one of our leaders called back.

Now, the people above us were waving their arms. They must have heard the shots and come out to see what was happening. They didn't want to be shot at, but from up there they could cheer us on enough to give us strength.

I slipped on a piece of ice and slid back several yards before stopping on a hard rock. I crawled, digging my hands into the partially frozen soil, to keep from sliding backward on the steep incline. My big boots made it hard to get a solid footing. I was getting tired. I had only one thought as the bullets flew passed me, I must make it to the top.

With bleeding hands and snow-soaked clothes, I finally reached the top. Crying and laughing I collapsed on the ground. I was not the first nor the last of our group to cross the border. Yet I was thankful than any for having succeeded in this treacherous journey to West Germany.

People from the Red Cross helped us to our feet. We walked to their station about a half mile away. I learned later that this station was erected to help those who might attempt to cross the border. The station was a short distance from the town of Bad Steben in West Germany.

After we were able to shower, I debated whether to give my real name or to continue in my boy disguise. I changed to my other clean set of underwear and wrapped a blanket around me to go to the washroom and launder my clothes.

As I came to the door, I saw a girl struggling with a man. She was trying o resist his attempts to molest her. A feeling of anger and disgust filled my body.

"It is the same everywhere," I said to myself. Men are the same everywhere. A girl traveling alone is not safe in the West either.

I stepped back and made a noise to let them know I was coming, then entered the room. The man did not stop his advances, thinking I was a boy. The girl continued to struggle. I dropped several wash bowls on the stone floor making a loud noise, and made them stop. The man laughed, he was not in the least embarrassed; the girl fled. I gathered up the bowls and started to wash the mud and dirt of f my boots and clothes.

Still wrapped in a blanket I stood in line for a bowl of soup. We were told that none of us could stay there more then three days, preferably less. We needed to make room for others who might follow. But take a good rest before you journey on. I sank into my bunk bed and fell asleep.

CHALLENGE OF THE BORDER
1947 - 1949

I slept all day at the Red Cross station, awakened to eat some dinner, then went back to bed and slept through the night. Dressed in dry cloths, I again stood in line for food. For the first time I could talk to others in our group. No one knew for sure who had been shot while we crossed as we were all nameless figures. The Red Cross only took care of the survivors and did not tell us what they had seen from above the hill. I was glad to be safe and asked no questions.

One of the Czechoslovakians explained that, the Russians had fired at random they had been very angry, he laughed. They probably found out from some of the guys they held behind, that we actually did come from the East, not from the West as we had told them. That was why they did not hesitate to shoot at us. "They were raving mad" laughed one of our leaders.

Grateful to have escaped injury, I bowed my head and thanked God for my safety. After my morning meal I explained to the Red Cross officials that Papa had been seen in an army hospital in Nuernberg. (Nuremberg) I was given a train ticket to Nurernberg and was told I could stay one more day in the shelter. Amazingly, new people arrived every night from the other side.

I wrote a letter to Mama telling her I was across the border and safe. In order to protect Mama, I avoided using my own name should the letter be confiscated. Red Cross people mailed it and informed me that the mail would get through to East Germany.

I walked into the town of Bad Steben. Small shops were open for business and merchandise was in the shop windows. People walking in the streets looked well nourished and content. What a difference, I was still in the same country, the same language. It seemed life in the two Germanies were like day and night.

The snow was melting in the sunshine. People stared at me as if I was just a pitiful creature. Timidly, I walked into the first shop, a bakery, where the smell of fresh bread was overwhelming.

For a while I just wanted to stand there and take it all in. When all the people in the place turned and looked at me, I was embarrassed and could not get a word out. I knew how to barter, but I had never learned how to beg.

The baker behind the counter did not hesitate and he pulled down an entire loaf of fresh baked bread from the shelf. "Here boy, you look hungry, have you just come from overthere?"

I nodded my head, when a lump in my throat prevented me from speaking. When I felt the bread in my hand I automatically pushed it inside my coat, curtsied, mumbled a "Thank you," then suddenly remembered that boys don't curtsy. His expression changed in astonishment. Everyone in the store laughed out loud as I ran out of the store as fast as I could.

Clutching my loaf of bread, I ran down the sidewalk. At first I feared investigation but, then, I realized where I was and guessed that it must have been all just a joke to them. Surely, if they really thought that I was not a boy they understood why.

Nobody followed me and I had a whole loaf of bread, all to myself. The fresh bread was still warm. Tears came to my eyes and I felt out of place not having to hide from suspicious eyes. The fragrance of the fresh bread was too much. I stopped and leaned against the wall and broke off a piece. It tasted heavenly. It was partly rye, not heavy commisbread like we ate in East Germany.

A soldier stopped and looked at me saying, "Don't eat bread alone boy.""Go into that butchery." He pointed, "They will give you meat. Just ask.

Meat! What a luxury. No one would give away meat, I thought. But he urged me on.

Finally I said, "I will try it."

I went into the butchery. I had not seen a butchery so well stocked for years. All those sausages. It was a sight--I stood there taking in the abundance of the meat display.

The man behind the counter said, "Here young soldier, have some of our daily special." Someone handed me a six-inch piece of tongue wurst. I stared and mumbled "Thanks" and remembered not to curtsy.

The butcher said, "Hey comrade, how is it on the other side?"

I replied, "People are still very hungry. Life is hard."

"Nothing has changed," he said nodding.

I stood there and ate the bread and tongue wurst.

"Here, have a glass of milk."

"Milk", I gasped. As I looked at the white liquid

always said, "You kids won't live long, you are war children. You just don't have the proper nourishment." If I could give Christine this milk I would do it instantly. Suddenly, having plenty and not

61

being able to share it with my family made me feel uneasy. In my mind I could see them hungry at the very moment I was eating.

Back at the Red Cross Station, I inquired about staying in West Germany. I was told that people born in East Germany must stay in East Germany. They are not refugees like the people from Silesia, Prussia, Sudetengau and other far East places. East Germans would not be permitted to permanently stay in West Germany. It was not until 1948 or 49 that residents of East Germany would also be accepted as political refugees. Still, I was sure many came and lied about their identity. I was only allowed to visit.

A Red Cross nurse said, "If we accepted East Germans, they would all come over here. No one would be left in Saxony and Thuringen. The Russians would completely take over the country just as they did with Latvia, Lithuania, and Estonia.

I did not know what was happening in those other countries she mentioned. I only knew that saying "No" meant much hardship to so many people. No one here could imagine what it was like under the Soviet rule. Here everything was so free and normal already, after that gruesome war.

I asked the local police the same questions and was given the same answers. "You may look for your father but you cannot have a permanent permit to live in West Germany."

I knew I must return to Saxony. I wrote another letter to Mama, explaining everything I had heard and seen. The Red Cross mailed it and I thought of little Christine. Had she gotten any milk since I left. Mama had my letter and gave me shelter until the next morning.

It was very early, as I took the first train to Nuremberg. People with friendly faces were saying "Good morning." No one on the trains looked as starved as the people in East Germany looked. The train was not overcrowded and I heard people talking gracefully about the Marshall Plan. Everyone thought it was a good thing for the beaten country. I vaguely remembered hearing something like this in East Germany and their propaganda talked against it. What horrible people those Communists were, pretending not to need help when everyone were starving.

The bombed out railroad station in Nuremberg was partially boarded up and reconstruction was underway. There were many people of different nationalities and American patrols (MPs) were walking around. Shops in the station were not open yet but the restaurant posted a menu in the window and stated when meals would be served. With little money and no ration cards, I was holding on to the rest of the food I had received the previous day. I boarded a streetcar going to Zirndorf, a suburb of Nuremberg. A hospital, containing German prisoners of war was located there. All afternoon I went from ward to ward looking for Papa. Upon learning of a ward where soldiers from the Russian front were being treated, I hurried to see if Papa was there. He was not--ic was now early evening and near curfew time. I approached a nurse and said, "I have no place to stay." She wrote an address on a slip of paper and warned me to get there before the curfew hour. As I left the hospital I came to a restaurant. I walked in and saw people eating big dinners, just like before the war. I was hungry and I guess I stared. A man took me by the shoulder and pushed me out. I was not dressed well enough to be in there anyway.

As I walked along wondering where I would rest for the night, I passed a place with a high brick wall around it. Curious, I walked around the wall and came to an open gate. Inside I saw a large courtyard where men were brushing and washing beautiful horses. This must be the American cavalry, I thought. I took a closer look. The men were talking to their horses and whistling cheerful tunes as they groomed them. No one paid any attention to me. I liked my boy disguise which allowed me freedom to do many things and still be almost unnoticed.

Across the courtyard was a three-story building that appeared to be quarters for the American men. A man's face appeared at an open upstairs window and he began calling out. One of the men with the horses nodded and gestured for me to look up. I looked around to just to be sure he was talking to me. I looked up at a very friendly face which I couldn't understand except for one word "chocolate."

"Oh yes, thank you." I answered in the few English words I knew.

The face disappeared and I returned to watching the men groom their horses. Feeling tired, I sat on the ground to rest. Soon the man with the friendly face came through a door carrying an armful of all kinds of sweet stuff. In the twilight of the evening with his shadow appearing to be eight feet tall and three feet wide, he looked so-o big! Enormous! Startled at his size, I jumped up and let out a yell. The man gaped at me in astonishment. As I turned around and ran out of there as fast as I could I heard loud laughter. But I had never talked to an American before nor even been close to one. He was really strange, much taller and different from the Russians and Germans or even the French and English POWs. Yet, his arms had been full of chocolate candies.

I hurried since I still had a few blocks to go to find the address the nurse had given me. Curfew was very soon. The address was on the fifth floor in an apartment building. A woman almost as old as my grandmother opened the door. I explained my situation and my search for Papa to this woman, since she seemed friendly. She said, "Yes, you may stay with me." Later I learned she was a widow. I felt secure with my new friend, Frau Berger, and thanked God that night for my safety. I slept soundly on a big feathertick under a feather comforter.

The next morning Frau Berger needed to get firewood and I offered to help. After eating breakfast, consisting of rye bread chicory coffee and jam, we set out to get a load of wood. We filled her four wheeled hand wagon, she pushed and I pulled until we got it back to her building. Carrying the wood to the fifth floor was quite a chore. However, she had promised me some food and lodging.

When we had our vegetable stew dinner she asked, 'Are you aware of the curfew, boy?" I nodded.

She continued, "The curfew starts as soon as it gets dark. The military police drive around in jeeps looking for all kinds of people. Entrances to buildings are locked just before curfew so don't run into a doorway thinking you can hide in there. The MPs and German police work together. People without proper IDs are sent back to the East. This could be real trouble for you.

They'll pickup anybody and take them to jail."

With Ortwin's ID I could not afford to be caught. I searched through hospitals all day with no luck. However, one day1 I went further into Zirndorf and found a camp for German POWs. American guards marched the POWs out in the morning and back in the late afternoon. I decided to wait until they returned.

With many hours to wait, I walked around talking to any likely person about where to locate missing persons. There were many POW camps, refugee camps, and more military hospitals. The Red Cross was busy with people who had lost citizenship from their home country. There were even camps for orphans who became lost while looking for their parents. Refugee camps were filled with families from the Eastern territories and housing was scarce. It would take a long time to bring order to things.

When I returned to camp the POWs were just entering the compound. As they passed, I slipped into their lines and marched in with them. Since I wore a sort of uniform too, except for the "POW' printed on the back and being somewhat smaller, I was hard to detect. A girl could never have done this, I thought. After marching a while, we were ordered to stand at attention. They closed the gates. I would worry about that fact later. Group leaders reported that all men were present then dismissed them. I walked among the POWs asking questions. Some men seemed surprised, some laughed.

"A kid has infiltrated! He's looking for his Dad."

"Where are you from? What is the name again?"

"What organization was he in?"

Many questions, but no answers. "I'm trying to find out if he is still alive. My mother has five children and she is waiting for him to come back from the war. He won't know that we're alive since we moved after being bombed."

"He may not be alive. He could be in another camp or in one of the Vet's hospitals. He might be in anyone of them."

As the men went inside they shrugged their shoulders and said they would like to help but no one knew anything to tell. Forlorn and disappointed, I walked slowly toward the gate. The guards saw me and I was taken into an office.

An American, I later learned first Sergeant, sitting behind his desk said, "You are in deep trouble boy." I did not understand him but I was worried by the tone of his voice. I told him, in German language, all there was to tell about my search for Papa. With the help of a translator he listened to my story.

"I could hand you over to the German Police!"

I could not hold back the tears. As he spoke to the translator, I was told he had decided to help me.

"Come," he said and led me to an American jeep with open sides. We got in. But I could run if things looked like he would hand me over to police. He drove through the streets and didn't say anything. Occasionally he whistled a tune. I hoped he would not find out who I really was because then he might not help me.

He stopped in front of a civilian apartment building. As he got out, he indicated I should stay in the jeep and that he would be right back. It was getting late and I knew I could not get to Frau Berger's home before curfew time.

Someone whistled. I looked up and saw the American motioning for me to come upstairs. I went up. A German girl stood in the open doorway and said, "Come in, boy. I am Sergeant James' fiancée, Anita. You may sleep on my couch tonight."

She looked at my worn out uniform and boots. Shook her head in disapproval that she had to look at such a mess as I was in and asked. "What's your name, lad?"

"Ortwin" I replied.

They gave me my first American "junk food." I saw and ate American white bread for the first time.

"This is like cake. Do Americans eat cake every day?"

"Don't be silly. It isn't cake, it's bread," she said.

I ate a whole sandwich. The fine grain melted in my mouth. I was excited by everything she gave me-corned beef, candy, chewing gum and chocolate. I inspected each piece as I ate it. "I n East Germany, any person caught by the police with items like this that are made in America, would get a jail sentence. I have much to tell Mama and my brothers."

They both smiled as I enjoyed the unusual food. Here I was, eating American food and the police did not know about it! Anita acted as though this amazing food was just every day stuff.

The guard had an "MP" on his uniform along with a lot of bright brass and I thought he must be someone really important. His boots were shined perfectly.

My oversized boots looked shabby and out of place here. I had worn the poorly fitting boots over two years now. "I hope to have shoes that fit some day," I said more to myself than to my hosts.

He looked so well dressed from head to foot yet the war had made many people into paupers.

"You can find everything under the sun on the West German black market," Anita explained. I wondered what black market she meant when her American friend must have brought everything she needed.

There are still many people with not enough clothing here in West Germany too. Mostly bombed out people or refugees. They come by the thousands and all want to stay here," she continued.

While she put away the dishes, she said, "Some people have relatives in the United States and receive gift packages and some even receive Care packages." I had no idea what "Care" meant and I was too tired to ask.

When she finished her work she went to sit with her boy friend and they began hugging and kissing in an open manner. He seemed embarrassed. He looked at me, said something, then tried to push her away. She kept clinging to him. I was sure he would enjoy her caresses if I had not been there. If she knew I was a girl she would probably kick me out.

"Do you want to smoke?" She interpreted what he said.

"Have one," he said, holding his cigarettes.

"I have never smoked," I replied. "Although I sold our own homegrown tobacco, I had never smoked it. My brothers do that for me to taste if it had the right fermentation and I even saw them. I use diluted homemade sugarbeet syrup diluted to prepare the tobacco."

They thought this was funny. I took a cigarette and watched him as he lit it. I inhaled and gasped! The stinging smoke in my lungs and throat made me cough. They laughed as they watched me try that first puff on a cigarette. "I do it later," I explained, laying the cigarette in the ashtray. "I thank you though for your help."

They were friendly and did not press me further. After a night's rest, I again thanked them for my bed and continued on with my search for Papa.

At one of the veteran's hospitals I was shocked to see so much suffering. Many patients had one or both arms or legs missing. I stared at one man's stumps and began to shake. The room felt warm and I took my hat and coat off, then unbuttoned the top of my shirt collar.

Startled, I heard, "Hey guys, my bride has come to see me." He roared with laughter, others shouted and whistled.

Scared of any questions, I left quickly. I walked rapidly back to Frau Berger's home. My thoughts were of Mama and of getting home. Frau Berger as she greeted me seemed relieved to see me. "I was so worried about you. I thought they had arrested you. I kept soup on the stove waiting for you."

I thanked her for thinking of me and proceeded to tell her about my activities and my desire to go home. "I doubt that Papa is here and I am needed at home."

"I understand. You are a very brave kid. I'll fix some food for you to eat on your way home."

With her gift of food1 I left for the railroad station where the Red Cross gave me a ticket to ride to the border. The station vas filled with people looking for missing family members. The Red Cross had hundreds of thousands of names on files of missing people. Although I did not know it then, it was to take twenty years and more for some families to be reunited and some have never found each other to this day.

People were talking about the Nuremberg trials, then in progress. I saw black market activities and could not participate. I talked to other travelers about how to cross the border. They were saying, "Don't go here." or "Don't go there." Some towns, they said were better to go through then others. "Go to Hof and then straight north." I soon knew I'd have to make up my own mind. This time I would be alone with no experienced Czechoslovakians to guide me. Word got around the waiting area that "a kid wants to make it back." Someone found an old map, pieced together with pins.

70

"Perhaps this will help," said an older man. I thanked him and sat down to study it. I boarded the night train so I would be at the border by dawn. Although the border was not that far, in these days the trains were always delayed. Besides, I wanted to spend a day on the western side near the border trying to find some food to take back home.

After we passed the city of Kronach only a few people were left in the passenger car. As the train sped toward the border I looked out of the window and knew spring was coming. I could smell it in the country air. I wished for lighter shoes and knew I'd be walking a long distance. The heavy boots hurt my feet.

When the train stopped I stepped down from the car and could see this was the end the tracks were actually cut of f. The earth had already forgotten right here, that once trains had run through and fro. Now the ground was covered with a thick growth of grass. Uncertain about where to go, I walked along a road into a farming area. I needed more directions than the map had provided I had to be very careful who I asked. Near the village of Stockheim I saw a woman in front of a farmhouse washing milk cans. I approached her. After explaining my needs, she faced me, put her hands on her hips and looked me up and down for a full minute. Then she said, 'Come in the house."

I followed her.

"I am a war widow. I have a sizable farm and my foreign help had gone home. I grow produce and it is hard to get help.

Even the refugees don't want to work. They would rather stay in the camps where they are fed for nothing. No one will work for so little money." She poured me a glass of fresh milk then sat down and watched me drink it.

She looked very serious and said, "How about you? Are you interested in work?"

"I'll have to think about ft." I was trying to grasp her situation in relation to my needs. "I need food more than money."

"I would let you go home every second weekend or so."

"But how can I go back and forth safely?"

"I know the forest master well, he may be able to help you."

"I don't see how it could work, I mean, to help you on a continuous basis."

"I'll give you as much food as you can carry."

To get food for Mama was a real temptation. To risk my life crossing the border again was another matter.

I hesitated, then said, "I'll help for a while. Let me think about coming back after I try crossing the border again. It is very dangerous on the other side." She nodded, she knew the border well.

I hesitated again, then took the plunge. "I must tell you something you don't know, I am a girl."

Her eyes widened and she looked at me more closely.

"These are the only clothes I have to wear. It is better for me to have people think I am a boy."

She nodded, then a twinkle came into her eyes. "You're okay. A real plucky kid. I admire your courage. My name is Theresa, what is yours?"

"Irene."

"Well, Irene, let's start by talking to the forest master."

As we walked through the village and up to the woods, I wondered why I completely trusted this brown curly haired woman

72

with a round face, and hands weathered by too much outside work. I could see she was intent upon having me work for her.

It turned out the forest master was a trusted friend. He agreed to go with me as far as possible to guide me toward and over the border.

The next two weeks were hard work! Theresa gave me some old clothes, skirts and blouses. Now I looked like a farm woman instead of a boy. I really did not care how I looked. My thoughts were on earning food. Up at five o'clock each day, I doused myself with cold water to wake up, then dressed quickly. After rinsing my mouth and combing my hair, I was ready for the day. While Theresa milked the cows I broke up a bale of hay and fed the horses. They nuzzled my sleeves as I fed them and as I pumped water and filled their watering troughs. We strained milk into large cans then carried them co the front of her property and set them on a wooden rack for the dairy truck to pick up.

After morning chores we went inside and drank milk and ate hearty pieces of bran bread spread with lard and cracklings. After breakfast we cleaned out the stalls and bundled straw from the threshing floor. We climbed up into the hay loft and kicked bales of hay through an opening to the courtyard below. Then dragged the bales into the stables. We cut them open and distributed them around the animals. But not before we cleaned out the stables from the old dirty stuff which we deposited on a pile outside, this was already manure for the fields in the spring.

The sun came out every day and melted the snow. Spring came in a rush, drying up puddles on the roads and in the fields. But it was still cold. The farmland would soon be dry enough to till for seeding. I stayed two weeks with Theresa, helping her with all the farm work. I wasn't hungry and the food made me stronger.

When it was time to leave for East Germany she said, "I'll pay you in money rather than food if you prefer." I told her, "When I get back home, food will be worth much more than money. The Reichsmark isn't worth anything anymore. My family is hungry and food is scarce."

She filled my knapsack and wooden suitcase with smoked sausages, salted bacon, baked goods, flour, butter, hard boiled eggs and many other good things. In this day and age my food supply was worth a fortune and my suitcase felt as heavy as bags of gold.

Early that rainy spring day Theresa walked with me to the forest master. He knew what was expected and picked up my heavy case of food to help me get started on my journey. "I'm afraid you will not come back." Theresa frowned. "I need your help so much."

"I will come back if it can be done," I promised.

The forest master carried the heavy load of food as far as he could toward the border, then stopped and said, "You're on your own from here kid. Be careful. Don't get caught, You know it's very dangerous."

"Thank you for your help, sir," I smiled bravely but my heart knew I feared the miles ahead.

"Stay to the right and you will see a fairly wide road when you get down this hill," said the forest master. "Keep hidden and stay in the brush. When you are sure no one is around, cross the road. Never mind the farm houses, they are probably empty. The East German authorities moved those families away from the border. This is no man's land. Avoid being seen until you see the town of Sonneberg. The train will stop there."

Down the rocky hill I went, stopping often to rest and listen. A gentle rain began falling and all seemed very quiet. I lifted my heavy load and zigzagged through the underbrush. Just as he had said, I saw the wide road at the bottom of the hill. At the least little noise I dropped to the ground and listened, holding my breath. I sat under a bush looking to my left side where I detected a narrow path. My action was not a moment too soon. A horde of Russian soldiers on horseback came in silence, riding right by me. They were so close, I saw their ready to shoot rifles glisten in the sun. I was able to see that they were Mongols. The Russian Army had many Mongolian soldiers in its midst. Luckily they did not see me, but I now realized how closely that border was watched. I felt tense and fearful, remembering my recent trip over the border.

Once I was sure they were gone I picked up my gear again.

The hill became very steep just above a flat clearing near the road. I stayed in the bushes as far as possible, then listened a long time before hurrying across the clearing and over the road. I rested in the shelter of some high bushes. I had read Karl May's books about the American Indian putting his ear to the ground to listen for footsteps that were some distance away. I tried it--all seemed quiet. - .

I struggled on with my heavy load, walking along the edge of the road near the underbrush. It was mid-morning and I hoped to get a train out of Sonneberg. I did not know the train schedule or the terrain between me and the railroad station. The ground was getting soft from the rain so I left the underbrush and walked along the hard road. It was less slippery but much more dangerous since I might be seen.

When I saw the Sonneberg railroad station in the distance, I felt confident and more relaxed. Hopefully, I would reach the station without mishap. I stayed on the road. Suddenly a World War II old car veered into sight! Two men were in it and they stopped. "Hey, kid, hop in. We know where you're coming from."

I gasped, fearing I'd lose everything I had worked for.

"How is it on the other side?"

I stared in amazement. In a real friendly fashion one of them got out and loaded my heavy suitcase into the car. They were Germans and in a hurry to get somewhere.

"We'll outsmart the Russian patrol by picking you up." I sank into the back seat next to my suitcase and asked, "Could you get me a ticket for the train? I have money."

I knew I would be suspected if I went into the station with all my luggage. They drove up to the station and got out. I waited by the car until the younger man returned with my ticket. "Good luck kid I hope you make it home safe." Suddenly I realized no one really cared much when people returned to East Germany.

As I lifted my heavy suitcase onto the train, a man walking along the tracks said, "We will not roll until afternoon but get on and find a seat."

People were already seated inside the train and some had waited since the day before. I learned there was only one train out of Sonneberg each week.

"You'll be lucky if you are not stopped by the Russians," a man warned me as he eyed my heavy suitcase.

So there would be more Russian control. I checked to see that my ID, with its official looking stamp was in my pocket. As scheduled, the train left and no Russian patrol had entered to check IDs. It was dark when we arrived in Zwickau and I had to change trains quickly. Many people were leaving the uranium mines for the weekend. They were crowding into the train, carrying heavy luggage and bumping into fellow travelers. A man tripped against my heavy suitcase. He swore, picked it up and threw it off the train. I jumped down after it. The heavy knapsack on my back buckled me to my knees.

I yelled, "I must have my suitcase!"

"Like hell you do! Look at our shins! There is no room", several men bellowed. We stood there packed in like sardines.

I lifted my suitcase up again and pushed it on the train, then jumped up to get a standing place. The suitcase was kicked off again. Fearing it would break, I screamed. After listening to more cursing, I was in tears.

"Give the kid his suitcase!"

The fight went on until the whistle blew. I was then off the train and my suitcase was on. The train started to roll. Train personnel, keeping a watchful eye to see that people did not cling to the outside of the train, were coming to prevent me from boarding. In desperation I ran and jumped up trying to get in before they closed the doors. A rough hand reached down and jerked me up into the overcrowded car. It took a few stations, till some people got of f, before I discovered my suitcase. All the passengers were men working in the uranium mines in Oberscilema, Schneeberg and Aue. This was a restricted area. It was the reason why I saw SO many police and Russians were on the platform.

When I changed trains in Glauchau it was much easier than before since I did not have to leave the tracks. I got of f and the train left. The next train pulled up and I boarded with ease. In Chemnitz I stayed at the tracks again and boarded a train to Niederwiesa. Outside the Chemnitz railroad station I knew only too well, would be the strong police force waiting for "hoarders." and hoping to confiscate foods stuff people brought almost home under great hardship. From Niederwiesa I had to walk about four miles then I would be home. Upon reaching Niederwiesa I half carried, half slid, the wooden suitcase into the luggage holding area. After seeing it stored safely on a shelf where it would be under the watchful eyes of the train personnel. I said, "I'll send my brothers for my suitcase." I turned and began walking, then I started to run - I was home at last.

"Irene! Irene! You've really come back." Mama's embrace was a haven of safety and wazitith.

Everybody cried with joy. Ortwin and Hartmut left immediately to get the precious food checked at the railroad station. What a story I had to tell. They all listened intently as I told my stories about West Germany.

"Mama, the Americans eat bread as fine and white as cake every day. They never eat that dark bread like ours. They have so much chocolate they want to give it away. They actually asked me if I wanted some! The bakery gave me a whole loaf of bread. Not like here, where we have to fight and beg for a slice of bread. The butcher gave me sausage without my asking for anything. I looked and looked for Papa and I couldn't find him." I was out of breath and very tired.

"Mama, I'll go back to the farm where I worked and bring lots of good food home."

"It's too dangerous. I'm afraid you will be killed!"

I knew we could use the food. Everyone looked so thin and hungry. With great pleasure, I watched their faces when we opened the knapsack and then the suitcase. A large piece of ham, and so much bacon. They had not seen this much meat since before the war.

Late in April I convinced Mama that I should try once more to cross the border. I was rested, my clothes were clean and Mama had once again cut my hair short. She hugged me as I left, saying, "God be with you Irene. Be careful." Tears streaked her thin worried face.

I planned to get to the border by nightfall. Although the distance could have been traveled in half a day, the zigzag pattern of travel which the Czechoslovakians taught me would take more time. I traveled west through Glauchau and down to Zwickau then I jumped on a boxcar that took me a little out of my way. I again bought a ticket to Plauen and tried to avoid the restricted area of Aue.

Near the border I saw so many police it seemed like an army. It crossed my mind that the authorities could be concealing the fact that our defeated country had an army again, dressed in police uniform.

By nightfall the train was rolling toward the town of Sonneberg. Before the city came into sight, the train stopped in the middle of nowhere and someone shouted, "Control!"

Police and Russians were boarding to look for unauthorized persons in the border area. By the time the train would arrive in Sneberg, all arrests would be already made. As they boarded, I jumped off. More police and guards were walking alongside the train with their backs to me. As they walked alongside the train, they shouted, that no one was allowed to get off or they would snot. Both sides of the train were encircled now and I knew I had jumped just in time. I tried to move away from the embankment and into some bushes. I had to find out where I was but it was pitch ark. No moon lit the way. Flattening myself against the ground I listened, hoping the blackness of the night would hide me.

Men were running and voices grew more excited and louder as they moved closer in my direction. They shouted and walked slower.

There must have been a few more people lucky enough to jump of f just in time. The Russians who had machine guns, were shooting into the air, to keep everybody else inside. Had they seen me? I didn't know. Slowly I turned my head, keeping most of my face covered. It was so dark I could only see the machine guns reflected by the lanterns. Apparently they were unaware of me.

Several people were taken of f the train and lined up. I felt sorry for them. Instead of a trip to the west and Freedom it would be for years, jail and hard times for them. Presumably, the police were not going to board the train again. This meant we must be within walking distance of Sonneberg.

The train pulled out and the police with their prisoners had marched on. I finally found myself alone, walking on the railroad tracks toward town. When the railroad station came into view I knew the direction I must go to cross the border. To avoid unexpected patrols I occasionally paused and listened into the night. I constantly watched for any movement in the darkness. Slowly, quietly, I walked around the town staying near the fields. I found the road that led me to the boulder strewn hill and climbed into West Germany. It must have been three in the morning when I arrived at Theresa's farmhouse. I sat on a bench in front of her house and fell asleep. Awakened by noises inside the house I knocked on the door. "Irene! You've really come back," Theresa cried. "I'm so glad. I was afraid you would not be able to get through.

"It is very dangerous, Theresa, and now there are so many police. I have been traveling all night and I am very tired."

While Theresa made hot broth and poured it on big chunks over dark bread, to make our flavored Breadsoup. I told her of my trip back home and about my hungry family. "Mama thinks things will soon be better but I see no signs of it. Everyone is hungry. It's a pity if only you could see the people over there. They must fight just for a slice of bread."

"Nothing will ever change over there," said Theresa. "You should consider staying here." Of course she knew the West German authorities would not let me stay and I would not abandon my family.

After some rest, I picked up where I had left off. Theresa and I worked outside all day then Theresa prepared the meals. There was plenty for us to eat.

One day Theresa said, "While you're here I can be a little like your mother." She smiled and patted my shoulder. I was happy for her friendship.

"Our Summer Festival is this weekend," Theresa explained. "What size dress do you wear?"

"Dress? I don't know what size. It's been some time since I had a dress to wear."

I could not picture myself in a pretty dress but I was very curious about her plans. I was sure a new dress in West Germany could only be found on the black market. To my delight, Theresa got me a beautiful dress. The skirt had little flowers on it and the top was black with a collar made from the same material as the skirt. I loved its wide skirt and the petticoat that came with it.

For the first time in years I had a pair of girl's shoes. They were not new but that made no difference. Red shoes, they were-sandals. So pretty and perfect and just my size. She gave me some underwear of her own and a string of red beads. As I looked in the mirror, I saw another person. I was a girl again. It felt good. If only Mama and my brothers could see me now. They did not know how good it was to be in West Germany.

"Thank you. Thank you so much, Theresa." I could not keep the tears from my eyes.

"Those stars in your eyes are thanks enough. Come now, after the evening chores we will go to the dance."

At the dance I felt out of place at fist. Soon Theresa introduced me to her friends and I learned many of them had already heard about me. I did not know how to dance but I saw that

— one of the musicians had a button accordion. At intermission I asked if I could play his instrument. He hesitated but then consented half heartedly. I thanked him and started to play, first two waltzes then two tangoes. Soon everyone was singing and tapping their feet. The other instruments followed me and it was one of the happiest times in many years.

Afterwards I sat with Theresa and her friends when a soldier still wearing parts of his uniform with civilian clothing, came toward me and said, "I'll teach you to dance if it kills me."

We laughed as he led me by the hand onto the dance floor. The floor was polished and slick and I slipped and tripped my partner. We both fell down. Laughing and joking, we scrambled to our feet. He then took me in a dance position and counted to the music, "One, two, three, four. Watch and step with me." He smiled and I followed. "One two three four and don't hesitate," he prompted.

It didn't take long at all until I could step to the rhythm of the music. First I learned to waltz, then to tango. What fun! After I learned a few steps, other boys asked me to dance. I did not even have time to drink a lemonade. I was getting warm but there was no stopping as I danced with partner after partner.

I felt light on my feet in the pretty red sandals. After learning the dance steps I felt relaxed and talked to my partners. I kidded with the fellows and they gave me tips on how to avoid the guards at the border. Most of them had lived in this area all their lives.

Our table was constantly surrounded by fellows wanting to dance or just talk. Theresa stood up and said pleasantly, "She must go home now, enough is enough. Tomorrow we have much work and church." As we left the fellows called "good night" from the doorway. Theresa and I laughed and talked all the way home.

Two weeks later I left at dawn to make my way back across the border. I left Theresa and the forest master at the top of the hill and descended the rocky slope, slipping often with my heavy load of food. Now and then I listened for several heartbeats, all I could hear was an occasional bird. At the bottom of the hill I crossed the clearing and the road to hide in the brush. I was breathing heavy from the strain of carrying my heavy knapsack and the old beatup suitcase. Everything was so quiet that I kept going in a hurry, rushing to catch the once-a-week train out of Sonneberg.

Just as I shouldered my heavy load, three riders on horses came silently out of the bushes. We spotted each other almost at the same moment. They whipped their horses to a gallop and were quickly in front of me--all Russians.

"Stoyt (Stop) they shouted. Since they were not sure I would understand Russian they started shooting in the air to emphasize that I stop. They jumped off their horses. Towering over me they shouted in Russian. I knew they were asking questions. I guessed they wanted to know what I was carrying and where I was coming from. I could not understand.

They ripped of f my knapsack and grabbed my heavy bags of food. I protested and they laughed and knocked me to tle ground. I hoped they would not discover that I was a girl, so I dared not get up as they cursed each other and fought over my food. I thought about Mama. We could have lived for weeks on all that food.

They must have decided to shoot me after taking my things. One of them took a big revolver out of his holster and checked the bullets. I could see he was trying to make himself angry so it would be easy to shoot me. He kicked me on the leg and shot the ground close to my head. I could hear the bullets strike the ground and smell the dust it made. I knew he was going to kill me.

My eyes were wide open and I wondered how it would be to die. Two of them started kicking me and shooting so close at me that I had to quickly move from one side to the other. Each blow from their boots sent sharp pains through my body. My arms and legs felt limp yet blow after blow struck my body. The blows came so fierce, suddenly I could not see. I must plead to stop them I thought. I felt all three of them worked me over at the same time and I knew, I soon would faint and die.

Suddenly I was looking down at myself lying on the ground. I was a spectator and nobody saw me, but I saw the whole scene. A dirty, bloody bundle, lifeless. Although three pair of boots kicked and stepped all over me I felt no pain. I knew instinctively that this was me and I thought, why is this happening?. They began playing Russian Roulette. Once they shot close to my head, then directly at it. They laughed as though they were having great fun. One soldier found his gun empty, started reloading and tried to hurry to get into the fun again. Then shots were heard nearby. A man on a horse was galloping toward us and I wondered, if he would run his horse's hooves over my body?. As he approached he shouted and shot into the air. He whirled his horse to a stop and the men stopped shooting.

Dismounting, he yanked me to my feet with such a force that I was conscious of being in my body again. As blackness came over me I felt my bowels move and I filled my pants. It was the last thought I had as I slid to the ground.

I must have lain there for a while for when I regained consciousness the man and my attackers were eating and dividing my possessions.

The man who was in command kept saying something that I understood as "He is a young boy. Let him go."

I opened my eyes to see one of the Russians staring down at me.

"Where do you belong?" He spoke in broken German.

I pointed toward the village I had- come from in West Germany. The pain in my body was returning with a vengeance and I wasn't sure if I could stand up and walk. I did not dare tell them my home was in Euba. I got on all fours then slowly stood up on my feet. My whole body hurt. All I wanted to do was to go to Theresa's house if I possibly could.

DAWEY! DAWEY! They all shouted angrily at me. Pointing toward the village where I came from. They knew without telling them that I came from the west. Nobody would have such good and abundant food in the east, but running up a hill in my condition was impossible. I walked, climbed, slipped, stood up and fell, all the while tears running down my face. After a few yards I leaned exhausted on a tree trunk. They started shooting into the air and I stopped for a while. When the shooting stopped I began climbing again. Once I was sure I was out of danger I sat down and rested behind a large rock.

Everything was taken except my ID card and some money I had put in my breast pocket. If they had searched me and discovered I was a girl from East Germany, they would have raped and killed me.

Finally, I reached Theresa's farmhouse. When she opened the door, she looked at me and became hysterical, crying and laughing at the same time.

"My dear girl, what have they done to you?"

"I thought they were going to kill me. When I left I had such beautiful white underclothing and look at me now."

"Come dear, you do need a bath." she said as she hurried to prepare some hot water.

As she gently washed my bruised body, Theresa said, "They worked you over badly. We ought to go to get you x-rayed you might have broken something".

"No I don't think so, my bones are made out of rubber" I joked. "I am alive and that is all that counts."

I hoped that I had not received some serious damage, my insides hurt so badly. "God was with me, Theresa, I know it." As she bandaged my wounds she said "One thing is for sure, you had a guardian angel that watched over you."

I rested a few days to partially recover from the deep bruises on my body. Theresa pleaded with me to stay with her, saying it was too dangerous to try to go back into East Germany. I wished I could stay. I was tired and things seemed hopeless but when I thought of Mama I knew I must return.

"My family needs me. They are so thin and hungry. You saw my skinny body. They too are starving and they have no one to help them. So many people are dying from hunger and typhoid. I just can't let this happen to them.

Theresa looked very sad and replied, 'You are a brave girl.'

"I'll be much more careful next time,' I replied.

One week later we got things together again. Friends in the village gave me an old knapsack and Theresa filled this and two cloth sacks, one for each hand. Laden with bacon, flour, butter, cheese, bread, boiled eggs and a bottle of oil. I set out one morning at dawn. By being extra cautious, I made it across the border and got to the railroad station on time. I did not want to risk running into the Russian patrol inside the station so I quickly boarded the train, planning to buy my ticket once I got on board. If questioned I'd say I lost my ticket.

Late that afternoon the train started to roll then stopped after traveling only a short distance. We waited there for hours. People talked quietly about anything except themselves. I surmised many of them were making the same sort of trip as I was. We were all carrying old luggage or sturdy sacks that appeared to contain food or black market ware. Most of us were thin. Our clothes were ill-matched, poorly fitted and dark in color. Few of us were wearing shoes of the right size.

By contrast the people in West Germany had enough to eat to keep a decent amount of flesh on their bones. Their shoes fit, and although their clothes appeared worn, they were c.ressed far better than anyone I had seen in East Germany. People in the West walked briskly with a sense of purpose in their lives and I saw no gaunt hollow-eyed people with the look of utter despair on their faces. Their faces displayed hope, hope that they would build up again.

American authorities, whether police or guards, were pleasant and courteous when conducting their work. The difference was so great I wasn't sure I could explain it to Mama.

The train started again and the realities of East Germany stood harshly before me. The next stop was Probstzella, not many miles from Sonneberg but still near the border and it was dark. A guard informed us the train would not run at night and we could not stay on it. This aroused tension and fear about where we were and where we would sleep. Since we were seeking transportation away from the border we considered ourselves somewhat safe among the numerous police guards.

The command to, "Find yourself a bed," told me not to expect a room by myself. My knapsack and two bags of food slowed me when I tried to follow the others seeking shelter. I barely managed to keep their shadowy figures in view as I followed. There were no street lights in this border town.

They stopped in front of what appeared to be a large inn.

A sign, lighted by a lamp on the wall of the building had the name of the Inn, " ZUR POST". The entrance was dark. As we approached, someone opened the door to reveal a lighted interior. We entered the main room. I turned and wanted to leave! The place was totally full with singing and beer-drinking uniformed policemen. I knew I could not find lodging out there in the dark. I had no choice but to go right into the "devils kitchen."

Timidly, I walked forward. Police were everywhere. They filled every table, laughing, talking, singing and drinking lots and lots of beer. They were of f duty and they did not want to notice people with their bags. Smoke filled the room and the man at the counter was busy filling large Beer stems with Pus Beer.

Ignoring my pounding heart, I held my head high and walked right up to the bar where a stout looking man handed over the beer to a waitress.

Like the people before and behind me, I asked, "Do you have a room?"

"Do you have a police permit? If not, we cannot give you a place to sleep."

"How do I get one?"

"Follow those people," he pointed. "They're going for permits. They will show you. It's about four blocks away," As I turned away from the counter I saw the people I had traveled with all day walking toward the door. I followed and we walked out into the night. After my eyes adjusted to the dark I realized I was far behind them again. I caught up with them as they were crossing a square. Worried about getting the permit, I hoped to talk to my fellow travelers about what to say but no one wanted to talk. Finally a man said, "Tell them as little as possible. That is all I can say."

Upon arriving we were told to wait on long benches in a brightly lighted hallway. No one could overhear reasons others gave for requesting lodging since each person entered a specified office, one at a time. I was fearful and uncertain when my turn came to be questioned.

"What is your reason for traveling?" asked the night officer.

"I visited in Sonneberg and I am on my way home, sir. You know how unreliable the trains are, often changing routes without scheduling, We have just arrived after long waits all day. I am stuck in a strange town."

He looked at me and his eyes narrowed. His face took on a new interest as he said, "You visited who in Sonneberg?"

"Some relatives. I'm on my way home." I swung my knapsack off my shoulders and placed it on the floor.

"What is your name?"

I hesitated, adjusting the straps on my knapsack. He got up, came around the desk and ripped the cap of f my head. I sensed he thought I was a girl?.

"DEIN NAME N" BISCHEN DALLYt" (Your name and be quick about it)

His face was so close to mine that if I perked my lips I would have kissed him. He shouted and I turned my face away. He grabbed me because he thought I would step back and away from him. I was surprised at that moment to see how ugly a man could be. I was outraged by his power over me. I dared not give my brother's name. I believed if I lied now he won't believe that I had visited relatives in

Sonneberg. He will ask me to open my baggage and I lose all my food again. Prison would be certain.

"Irene," I hurried to add. "I have to travel as a boy. You have no idea what men do to girls. It's much safer to travel as a boy."

"Only If you can get away with it," he smiled as he returned to his desk. 'I'll give you a pass for tonight but never let me catch you again." He was shaking his head, while he wrote out my permit.

'Thank you, sir." I curtsied and walked outside.

Suddenly I felt relaxed and free from tension. A permit to sleep in the hotel! How lucky! I felt as if I was flying as I returned to the Inn. When I got there I walked right into that room full of police.

We were charged a few marks for the night and then were directed upstairs into a large long room containing about forty narrow beds, twenty on each side. Men and women were not separated and the light stayed on all night. Our beds were meticulously clean, narrow like a soldier's bed with thin mattresses and white sheets. White pillows and field grey blankets completed our sleeping accommodations.

We were checked and permission slips were relinquished. The police counted us again, then counted the slips. Each of us was assigned a bed. I tied my knapsack and two bags of food to the headpiece of the bed. I was not worried someone would steal it. Unless the smell of the food made someone very hungry. The light in the room was very bright. At the entrance of the long room was a desk where a policeman sat all night, keeping control over us I thought. Getting into bed with most of my clothes on, I pulled my cap over my forehead to keep the light out of my eyes. Not even the noise from the boisterous policemen downstairs kept me from a deep sleep.

It was still dark outside when we were ordered to get up. The light was still on and we were hurried into a washroom and given a few minutes to use toilets, rinse our teeth and wash up. It was always, Hurry! Hurry!. —

After counting us again we were marched downstairs. I could just imagine the trouble and delay that would occur if there had been one too many of us, or worse, one less. — Again, " Hurry! Hurry!" they shouted as we were rushed through the dark to a waiting truck.

I saw Russian guards with those awful machine guns hanging on their backs. Out of the truck and into the train, we had to move fast. Now it was DAWAY! DAWAY! the Russian call for HURRY!. It was still dark and I had no idea what time it was. Those with watches a kept the time to themselves as it was not wise to show a watch when Russian soldiers were around. They were everywhere, walking up and down the platform impatiently hurrying us on. No one was allowed to stay behind.

"Get on the train immediately!" shouted the police repeatedly. They wanted us all away from the border as quickly as a possible. The shouting of orders was continuous and loud. Their departing shout was, "If you come back here you can expect to be under arrest!"

The train was dark and crowded. Men were standing. No one spoke as we jostled for places to sit or stand holding our ungainly bags as close as possible. The train moved then stopped. After this a action was repeated several times, we finally pulled out making our way to Thueringen. When we stopped at Saalfeld several people got off and those of us remaining were able to find a seat. To our dismay, more people got on and the train was once again filled beyond capacity. Many stood between cars and I heard bodies on the roof. I hoped they would not fall when the train went through the tunnels.

I changed trains once, to mainstation (Hauptbahnhof) Chemnitz. The Dresden train which stopped in Niederwiesa, from that station I would walk home.

When I saw Mama's worried face I wept. "I cannot bear to let you go again, Irene. It's too risky."

"I know, Mama, it is very dangerous and right now all I want is some rest." I was too tired to think clearly.

In the days ahead I told Mama about the Russian patrol on horses and how I had gone back to Theresa's farm. I told her of the increasing numbers of police in the border area. We weighed those risks compared to working on the farm for food in East Germany and scouring the country for food by riding the freight cars and bartering in the black market.

"The food you bring makes a big difference but the danger is too great. we need more food than we can get from our work here on the farm. The boys work every hour they are not in school for almost nothing and they are hungry." Mama shook her head and sighed. "Surely this cannot last much longer. If the harvest from our garden would amount to anything, we could dry some stuff for the winter."

Of course I knew Mama was missing all her canning supplies she had lost in the bombing. Now it was impossible to buy these items. I was convinced the risks I took paid off in more than just food for our family and for some unknown reason the adventure of evading the police by traveling like I did was more than a little fascinating.

"The trade schools are not organized yet Mama. Until the schools offer classes again, I think I should try to bring food from West

93

Germany. In a few days I'll go into Chemnitz and see how things really are."

Mama thought this was a good idea. Perhaps she would even relent and approve of my continued trips into West Germany. A few days later I took two raw potatoes and a few ounces of bacon and walked into Chemnitz. I needed money for train fares and the black market would provide me with it.

In Chemnitz changes were coming very slow. Day by day and brick by brick the brave rubble women (Truemmerfrauen) were cleaning and sorting the debris from the bombing. With their hands wrapped in rags or old gloves, they pushed their heavily laden lorries on tracks through the streets. Clearing was being done but no construction had began. There was no evidence of any new materials to repair anything and cardboard still covered the windows.

Nevertheless, as meager as East Germany's efforts were, I knew deep inside me the vigor and industriousness of our people could return. German people are strong and thrifty.

A restaurant in the inner city was trying o reopen, guests were sitting at tables in the open air with a view of the rubble. Its menu, which hung on a rock outside, announced that by bringing two large potatoes and paying in Reichsmark one could get a bowl of soup. I stood in line after forfeiting my potatoes and five Reichsmark for a slip of paper. After a long wait I was summoned to a table where others were already eating. The waiter, carrying a huge tray of bowls and acting like a military figure of authority, landed a bow), of soup in front of me. No utensils were provided. I ate with a spoon which I always carried with me like anyone else, in case something eatable could be unexpectedly found.

I looked down at a bowl of watery soup, cabbage I guessed by the aroma plus, some grits and potato pieces. It was seasoned with spices to make it tasty. There was no meat in my serving and I felt sure the kitchen had no meat to serve. It was edible and it filled my stomach. When the waiter saw my bowl was almost empty, he ordered me to eat faster so others could be seated. As I saw him serving others in this same fashion, I thought of how lavish it was before the war and new how humble and timid we had become in our defeat. We were now pitiful creatures struggling to keep alive.

I walked from the restaurant, past the women working in the rubble, to the Schocken Department Store. It was now government property. Advertising merchandise was unheard of and the department stores stood empty and alone. No people around even though it was not bombed.

As late as 1948 some flimsy limited amounts of merchandise were seen. The entire store had no more than a dozen shirts, blouses, coats and other assorted clothing. It was sold out in minutes and the people that waited in line since the day before, I even slept on the pavement, had to go home with nothing. People living and working outside the city, had no chance to buy anything. I walked to the railroad station where most of the black market activities took place. I received 200 Reichsmark for a pound of smoked bacon, more than enough to pay for my train fare to and from West Germany and still leave some money for Mama.

During the early months of 1947 and into the spring of 1948 I made many uneventful trips back and forth across the border between East and West Germany. Each time I made a trip the number of police seemed to be increasing. This was before the land mining was done.

95

At that time the communists used heavy police patrols but many people were still able to slip through the borders. When caught they were sent to the Bautzen Penitentiary where they received eight to ten year sentences all because they wanted to cross the border. I know this from a distant relative who disappeared and also by reading Walter Kempowski's Book "Im Block". He spent many years in Bautzen.

Winter, though bitter cold, was the safest time for those secretive trips. Russian border guards were not so keen on staying outside for many hours waiting to catch people in this subzero weather. The guards preferred card playing and the warmth of their little "watch houses."

I had learned what trains to catch and how to avoid crowded rail road stations. I studied train schedules coistantly to avoid long waits. I learned to act as though I lived in whatever village I was in and to avoid the suspicious eyes of the police. The darkest nights with cloud cover from the moon gave me a feeling of greater safety when traveling in the country. I put my ear to the ground and listened often for the footsteps of men or their horses on patrol. I learned to distinguish noises but sometimes I mistook a running deer for a border patrol guard. It was easier to hear clear sounds during the winter months.

Mama once said I developed a keen sense of hearing and sight since I always heard the faintest whisper and saw the smallest movement in the house. I was not the only one to cross the border repeatedly in search of work and food. Sometimes I saw the same faces as I repeated my dangerous journeys. Some people who crossed the border at other places did not return.

It became easy to identify people approaching the border for the first time. They were apprehensive and some tried to hang on along my trail. Since this increased the danger, I tried to shake them just as the two Czechoslovakians once tried to lose me on my first trip.

Clothing to keep warm was a constant problem. One day a helpful villager in West Germany gave me an Eisenhower jacket. What a combination, the black SS uniform trouser topped by an Eisenhower jacket. It fit just fine. I bought a pair of worn men's shoes--a little large but a welcome change for warm weather. Theresa gave me some dresses but I always left them at her house.

Christmas, of 1947, was bleak but there was enough food to keep us alive. The distance and cold weather kept us from going into Chemnitz to worship. Instead, we attended services in the village church. We slowly realized that Papa might not be alive.

On a winter day early in 1948, I bought my last train ticket at the railroad station in Chemnitz to go toward the border of West Germany. I was hastily stuffing a sandwich into my mouth when a small boy came toward me, his hands outstretched for my food. He looked so starved, his large sad eyes made me stop eating and I gave him the other half of my sandwich. He consumed it immediately. I opened my knapsack and gave him another sandwich I was carrying for a later meal. He did not even smile but his dark hollow eyes were full of thanks as he ate the bread in big bites. I closed my knapsack and walked away with a lump in my throat, thankful to be able to bring food to my family.

In Glauchau I waited hours for another train. Russian soldiers making their rounds spotted me leaning against the wall outside of the station.

"You have wristwatch?"

I shook my head. Three of them closed in around me. Two of them grabbed my arms and rolled up my sleeves, looking for a watch I didn't have. One of them turned me around and twisted my arm high up my back.. The intense pain made me feel faint and I buckled down on my knees. There was no one around to help me. As a German would be much too afraid to interfere. If he breaks my arm, I'll have to go back home, I thought.

One of the soldiers, angry at not finding a watch, started to search my pockets. I flattened myself on the station platform.

He kicked me in the ribs and I doubled up in pain. Then they spotted another victim and left me after one more blow with a boot. I lay there until the pain stopped and thanked God my arm was not broken. The Russians were apparently only looking for watches. They seemed to think every German had a wristwatch. In those days it was better to leave a watch at home.

As the train arrived a compartment opened revealing two Russians fighting with each other. Plunk! Several boxes fell out and broke open. Cartons of German cigarettes, made in Dresden, tumbled out onto the ground.

I and several others did not hesitate, we each picked up as much as we could, stuffing our pockets full. One girl looked up at me and said, "Oh!, I just want to help them get their cigarettes.

"So do I," I said and quickly jumped on the slow moving train. I checked my pockets--twenty some packages of cigarettes. They were made of the finest Bulgarian tobacco, considered to be the best in East Germany. I tucked them into my knapsack and pretended I knew nothing about them.

When I arrived at Theresa's home, a refugee was living with her. It was much better for her to have two people working on her farm and it made it easier for me to tell her that I could not come back again. Schools would be opening soon and I planned to study nursing.

During the final few weeks of work the village people learned that I would riot return. They showered me with gifts. I could not carry all of them, shoes, dresses, underwear and generous gifts of food. I mailed several boxes containing clothing, silk stockings, a whole sack of flour and the cigarettes I had picked up in East Germany. All nonperishable foods I could possibly get mailed of f and all arrived safely in Euba.

"I'll try to send your family packages in the future," Theresa promised.

The words "thank you" seemed extremely inadequate when it was time to say goodbye to Theresa and to those I had made friends with. On another rainy day I walked, heavily laden with food, down the rocky bill and out of their lives.

My last trip was carefully timed. I was able to avoid the increasing police activity and arrived home under the shelter of darkness as I had done countless times before.

Continue reading Irene's story in the third and final book – My Escape to Freedom.

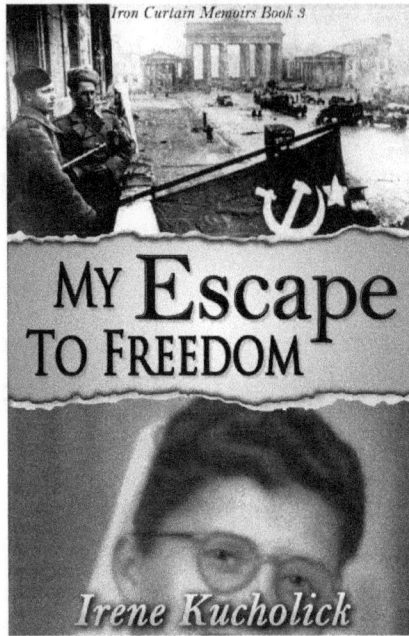

Iron Curtain Memoirs Book 3

MY Escape
TO FREEDOM

Irene Kucholick

If you missed Book 1, check out My WWII Childhood.

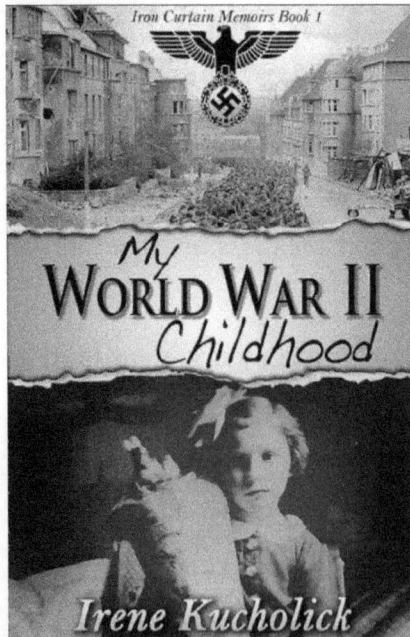

Iron Curtain Memoirs Book 1

My
WORLD WAR II
Childhood

Irene Kucholick

www.ingramcontent.com/pod-product-compliance
Lightning Source LLC
Chambersburg PA
CBHW031537040426
42445CB00010B/582